Black Diamond

The Story of the Negro Baseball Leagues

Patricia C. McKissack and

Fredrick McKissack, Jr.

SCHOLASTIC INC.   NEW YORK · TORONTO · LONDON · AUCKLAND · SYDNEY
MEXICO CITY · NEW DELHI · HONG KONG

No part of this publication may be reproduced in whole or in part, or stored in a retrieval
system, or transmitted in any form or by any means, electronic, mechanical, photocopying,
recording, or otherwise, without written permission of the publisher. For information
regarding permission, write to Attention: Permissions Department, Scholastic Inc.,
555 Broadway, New York, NY 10012.

ISBN 0-590-68213-X

Copyright © 1994 by Patricia C. McKissack and Fredrick McKissack, Jr. All rights reserved.
Published by Scholastic Inc. SCHOLASTIC and associated logos are trademarks and/or
registered trademarks of Scholastic Inc.

24 23 22 21   11 12 13 14 15 16/0

Printed in the U.S.A.   40

First Scholastic paperback printing, September 1998

Praise for Patricia C. McKissack
and Fredrick McKissack, Jr.'s

Black Diamond
The Story of the Negro Baseball Leagues

"This book ... makes the trip with style.... oral histories from surviving
players add startling depth to descriptions ..."   —*Booklist*

"[an] exceptional narrative of a vivid era in U.S. sports history. Spirited,
entertaining, and well-researched, this is an eye-opener ..."
                                                —*The Boston Sunday Globe*

"Here's an engaging account that traces the national pastime...."
                                        —*The New York Times Book Review*

"... a winner ... this book gives a comprehensive and compelling history."
                                                        —*Chicago Tribune*

"[the authors] combine eloquent writing with meticulous research."
                                                —*National Black Review*

"This panoramic look at Black baseball ... puts athletes like Rube Foster,
Josh Gibson, and Lyle 'Toni' Stone ... into historical perspective. Classy
pictures and a time line add to the book's value."   —*Essence*

~~~~~~

A Coretta Scott King Honor Book
A Notable Children's Trade Book
in the Field of Social Studies
~~~~~~

A new direction in nonfiction.

POLARIS

To Dave M., John K., Chuck X., Kevin C.,
and the Opera Dogs

CONTENTS

◆

The Shutout

THE history of baseball is difficult to trace because it is embroidered with wonderful anecdotes that are fun but not necessarily supported by fact. There are a lot of myths that persist about baseball — the games, the players, the owners, and the fans — in spite of contemporary research that disproves most of them. For example, the story that West Point cadet Abner Doubleday "invented" baseball in 1839 while at Cooperstown, New York, continues to be widely accepted, even though, according to his diaries, Doubleday never visited Cooperstown. A number of records and documents show that people were playing stick-and-ball games long before the 1839 date.

Albigence Waldo, a surgeon with George Washington's troops at Valley Forge, wrote in his diary that

The all-white Cincinnati Reds in 1869.

soldiers were "batting balls and running bases" in
their free time. Samuel Hopkins Adams (1871–1958),
an American historical novelist, stated that his grandfather "played base ball on Mr. Mumford's pasture"
in the 1820s.

Although baseball is a uniquely American sport, it

was not invented by a single person. Probably the game evolved from a variety of stick-and-ball games that were played in Europe, Asia, Africa, and the Americas for centuries and brought to the colonies by the most diverse group of people ever to populate a continent. More specifically, some historians believe baseball is an outgrowth of its first cousin, *rounders*, an English game. Robin Carver wrote in his *Book of Sports* (1834) that "an American version of rounders called *goal ball* was rivaling cricket in popularity."

It is generally accepted that by 1845, baseball, as it is recognized today, was becoming popular, especially in New York. In that year a group of baseball enthusiasts organized the New York Knickerbocker Club. They tried to standardize the game by establishing guidelines for "proper play."

The Knickerbockers' rules set the playing field — a diamond-shaped infield with four bases (first, second, third, and home) placed ninety feet apart. At that time, the pitching distance was forty-five feet from home base and the "pitch" was thrown underhanded. The three-strikes-out rule, the three-out inning, and the ways in which a player could be called out were also specified. However, the nine-man team and nine-inning game were not established until later. Over the years, the Knickerbockers' basic rules of play haven't changed much.

In 1857–1858, the newly organized National Association of Base Ball Players was formed, and baseball became a business. Twenty-five clubs — mostly from eastern states — formed the Association for the purpose of setting rules and guidelines for club and team competition. The Association defined a professional player as a person who "played for money, place, or emolument (profit)." The Association also authorized an admission fee for one of the first "all-star" games between Brooklyn and New York. Fifteen hundred people paid fifty cents to see that game. Baseball was on its way to becoming the nation's number-one sport.

By 1860, the same year South Carolina seceded from the Union, there were about sixty teams in the Association. For obvious reasons none of them were from the South. Baseball's development was slow during the Civil War years, but teams continued to compete, and military records show that, sometimes between battles, Union soldiers chose up teams and played baseball games. It was during this time that records began mentioning African-American players. One war journalist noted that black players were "sought after as teammates because of their skill as ball handlers."

Information about the role of African Americans in the early stages of baseball development is slight. Several West African cultures had stick-and-ball and running games, so at least some blacks were familiar with the concept of baseball. Baseball, however, was not a popular southern sport, never equal to boxing, wrestling, footracing, or horse racing among the privileged landowners.

Slave owners preferred these individual sports because they could enter their slaves in competitions, watch the event from a safe distance, pocket the win-

Some escaped slaves joined the Union forces where baseball was played by both white and black soldiers.

Baseball is being played behind a group of Civil War troops.

nings, and personally never raise a sweat. There are documents to show that slave masters made a great deal of money from the athletic skills of their slaves.

Free blacks, on the other hand, played on and against integrated teams in large eastern cities and in

small midwestern hamlets. It is believed that some of the emancipated slaves and runaways who served in the Union Army learned how to play baseball from northern blacks and whites who had been playing together for years.

After the Civil War, returning soldiers helped to inspire a new interest in baseball all over the country. Teams sprung up in northern and midwestern cities, and naturally African Americans were interested in joining some of these clubs. But the National Association of Base Ball Players had other ideas. They voted in December 1867 not to admit any team for membership that "may be composed of one or more colored persons." Their reasoning was as irrational as the racism that shaped it: "If colored clubs were admitted," the Association stated, "there would be in all probability some division of feeling whereas, by excluding them no injury could result to anyone . . . and to keep out of the convention the discussion of any subjects having a political bearing as this [admission of blacks on the Association teams] undoubtably would."

So, from the start, organized baseball tried to limit or exclude African-American participation. In the early days a few black ball players managed to play on integrated minor league teams. A few even made it to the majors, but by the turn of the century, black players were shut out of the major leagues until after World War II. That doesn't mean African Americans didn't play the game. They did.

Black people organized their own teams, formed leagues, and competed for championships. The history of the old "Negro Leagues" and the players who barnstormed on black diamonds is one of baseball's most interesting chapters, but the story is a researcher's nightmare. Black baseball was outside the mainstream of the major leagues, so team and player records weren't well kept, and for the most part, the white press ignored black clubs or portrayed them as clowns. And for a long time the Baseball Hall of Fame didn't recognize any of the Negro League players. Because of the lack of documentation, many people thought the Negro Leagues' stories were nothing more than myths and yarns, but that is not the case. The history of the Negro Leagues is a patchwork of human drama and comedy, filled with legendary heroes, infamous owners, triple-headers, low pay, and long bus rides home — not unlike the majors.

CHAPTER

1

Play Ball

BLACK baseball's beginnings are difficult to pinpoint. Seemingly, African Americans played on the same teams with whites and on all-black teams against whites during the early days of baseball. Although documentation is sketchy, there is enough information to show that blacks formed teams that played for local championships. Attending a baseball game in the late 1860s was a premier social event in black communities in the east and midwest. Early records show that in October 1867, the Uniques of Brooklyn hosted the Excelsiors of Philadelphia in a championship game to determine "the champion of colored clubs."

The integrated crowd cheered as the Excelsiors marched around the field led by a fife and drum corps.

The Brooklyn Daily Union described it as a festive but orderly affair:

> *"These organizations are composed of well-respected colored people, well-to-do in the world . . . and include many first-class players; and we trust that none of the 'white trash' who follow white clubs will be allowed to mar the pleasure of these social colored gatherings."*

But that's not the nature of baseball. It is not surprising that the game was "marred by arguments and called after seven innings because of darkness." The Excelsiors beat Brooklyn, 37–24.

The first professional baseball league was formed in 1871. It was a player-run organization called the National Association of Professional Baseball Players. It was structured much like the old Association. The Pythians, an all-black team from Philadelphia, applied for admission in this organization. In 1869, the Pythians had been the first all-black team to take the mound in competition against the all-white City Items, beating them, 27–17. But the new National Association held with the ruling of the former NABP, and rejected the Pythians' application. None of the original charter clubs in the National Association were black.

Black clubs continued to form and compete with themselves and with clubs outside the Association. Then in 1876, the National League of Professional

Base Ball Clubs was organized. William A. Hulbert of the Chicago White Stockings was one of the founders of the National League (NL) and served as its president from 1877 until his death in 1882. Again, no all-black clubs were admitted. And while there was no written policy restricting blacks from playing in the league, it was generally agreed among the club owners that none would be signed up.

During this time there were several African-American professional ball players who left their mark on baseball, even though they were not given the opportunity to perform in the large arena of the National League. Among these trailblazers were two outstanding players — Bud Fowler and Fleet Walker.

John Jackson was born in 1858 in upstate New York. Later he changed his name to John Fowler, but to most people, especially his teammates, he was known as "Bud."

Bud Fowler grew up in Cooperstown, New York, where the Baseball Hall of Fame would one day be located. There's a story that was told among ball players about a conversation between two baseball fans:

Fan 1: *Man, have you heard? They're opening a Baseball Hall of Fame in Cooperstown, New York.*

Fan 2: *Well, isn't that nice. They put it in Cooperstown to honor the great Bud*

> *Fowler. That's where he grew up, you*
> *know?*
>
> *Fan 1: Now you know them white folks*
> *wouldn't put the Hall of Fame up in*
> *honor of no black ball player.*
>
> *Fan 2: Well they should! Bud Fowler was one*
> *of the best players that ever held a bat —*
> *black or white.*

Even though the praise given to Bud Fowler was well deserved, he is not in the Baseball Hall of Fame.

Fowler spent twenty-five years traveling a bumpy road of triumphs and disappointments. He played for fourteen teams in nine leagues, and batted about .300 each season. He led the Western League in triples in 1886, yet he was never picked up by a National League team.

He had learned to play the game as a boy, and was good enough by age twenty to turn pro. In 1872, he joined a team in New Castle, Pennsylvania, where he was the only black pitcher. Soon after, he moved to a local team in Chelsea, Massachusetts, where he defeated the National League's Boston team in a 2–1 victory in an exhibition game. He distinguished himself three times on the mound for the Lynn Live Oaks in the International Association, the first minor league. Although he was as good as any of his peers, Fowler was not picked up by any of the major league teams, due to racial prejudice.

Bud Fowler (back row center) shown here with the Keokuk team.

Like many of the early players, he played more than one position. Fowler was a good pitcher, but he shifted to second base. The pitching position was coveted by white players, so he figured that by shifting to second base there might be more opportunities open to him.

The Sporting Life, a newspaper of sports in the late nineteenth century, summarized Fowler's career during the 1885 season.

"Fowler, the crack colored second baseman, is still in Denver, Colorado, disengaged. The poor fellow's skin is against him. With his splendid abilities he would long ago have been on some good ball club had his skin been white instead of black. . . . Those who know, say there is no better second baseman in the country."

Moses Fleetwood Walker, better known as Fleet Walker, was born October 7, 1857, in Mount Pleasant, Ohio. His father, Dr. Moses Walker, moved the family to Steubenville, Ohio, when Fleet was a boy. Ohio was a vital connection in the Underground Railroad, a network of abolitionists who helped runaway slaves reach freedom. Having never been a slave, Fleet grew up with a strong self-image, but he understood the suffering of those who had been enslaved.

While at Oberlin College, one of the first integrated colleges in the United States, Fleet and his brother, Weldy Walker, helped start a varsity baseball team. Later the brothers played together at the University of Michigan, where Fleet made a name for himself as a catcher.

In those days the ball was caught bare-handed, and there were no chest protectors or face masks. Catchers were often the first to suffer injuries, some of them very serious. Fleet soon learned just how dangerous his position could be in a bigoted situation.

After his college career ended, Fleet turned pro and signed with a minor league team in Toledo, Ohio. After his first year, Toledo joined the American Association (AA), which was a major league. The AA had no color barriers. Although the AA was in its infancy and the National League was much more prestigious, Walker is credited with being the first black major league player.

His debut in the majors evoked reactions ranging from curiosity to contempt. While he received a warm welcome and cheers for his skill behind the plate in Baltimore and Washington, D.C., he was booed in Louisville. In Richmond, Virginia, Toledo's manager was sent a message signed by seventy-five men who threatened to mob Walker if he took the field. And, on August 10, 1883, Cap Anson (a Hall of Famer), player and manager of the Chicago White Stockings, also threatened to cancel an exhibition game with Toledo if Fleet played.

The Toledo manager, Charlie Morton, called Anson's bluff and put Walker in the lineup. The game was played without incident.

Walker broke a rib in July 1884 and played sparingly for the rest of the season. Even though he had earned respect among the players and the fans, at the end of the season the Toledo team folded.

Toledo's crack pitcher, Tony Mullane, said Walker was "the best catcher I ever worked with," but he didn't feel that way when they were teammates. Mullane admitted, "I disliked a Negro, and whenever I had to pitch to him, I used anything I wanted without looking at his signals."

Meanwhile, Weldy Walker, Fleet's younger brother, played six games with Toledo in a series against Indianapolis in 1884. After Toledo folded, the AA closed its doors to black players.

Fowler and Walker were only two of several early

Fleet Walker (middle row far left) and his brother Weldy (back row second from the right) played on the varsity team at Oberlin College in 1881.

ball players who deserve recognition. In 1887, eight of the best black players went into the minors, playing in the newly formed International League.

In 1887, it seemed that baseball might succeed at dropping the color barrier. The International League (IL), consisting of teams in Canada and upstate New York, accepted black players; among them were Fowler who went to Binghamton and Walker who signed with Buffalo. Joining them in the IL were Buffalo infielder Frank Grant, whom *The Sporting Life* called "a great all-around player," and pitcher George Stovey, who won thirty-three (thirty-five?) games and lost fourteen that year — which is still an International League record.

Although their performances were outstanding in the field, on the mound, behind the plate, and at bat, the black players were still not accepted on the merit of their skills. They endured fans calling them "the nigger pitcher" or the "coon catcher," newspaper headlines declaring, "Colored Players Distasteful," and *The Sporting Life* asking, "How far will this mania for engaging colored players go on?"

On the field the indignities didn't stop. Opposing pitchers often threw beanballs at black batters. An unnamed white player remembered, "Fowler used to play second base with the lower part of his legs encased in wooden guards. He knew that about every player that came down to second base on a steal had it in for him."

Frank Grant (bottom row second from the right) with the
Buffalo Club, International League ca. 1888.

But being spiked wasn't as painful as being shunned
by fellow players. Grant narrowly escaped a beating
from his teammates, and the Binghamton squad refused to take a team picture with Fowler and threatened not to play if he remained on the team. The
management caved in under the pressure, and Fowler
was released by the club.

Then in July 1887, the IL directors decided that since white players had misgivings about blacks and had threatened to leave the league if something was not done, no more contracts would be offered to black ball players. The color line was being drawn. Although the few blacks who were still playing in the IL at the time were not immediately dismissed, the day was drawing nearer when each one would be shut out of minor league play, too.

George Stovey was slated to pitch against the Chicago White Stockings in an exhibition game in Newark. Chicago was the top team in the majors at the time, but everybody knew that Stovey was the best pitcher around. It was rumored that the New York Giants were showing some interest in him. After all, baseball was a business and if Stovey could help them win games, then the New York club was willing to forget about color. But would the Giants break the "gentleman's agreement" that had existed between National League owners and sign a black player?

We can only guess about what might have happened. Cap Anson, Chicago's player-manager, who had tried to bar Fleet Walker from an exhibition game with Toledo a few years earlier, secretly threatened to call the game if Stovey played. "Get that nigger off the field," he said, spitting on the ground. Once again management gave in to pressure. They issued a pregame statement removing Stovey from the lineup. "Due to illness" was given as the cause, but Stovey wasn't ill. Months later, the real reason was revealed in the media, but the shutout of black players continued.

By 1888, there were still five blacks in the integrated IL. Stovey had been dropped, and it was a particularly difficult time for Frank Grant. Although he had a very impressive record with Buffalo — a .326 batting average and eleven homers in ninety-five games — Grant was hassled by opposing players who tried to cleat him with their spiked shoes. Although he, too, wore wooden shinguards, he ended up having to abandon his second-base position. Yet, he was forced to muff balls (to drop the ball intentionally) for fear that he might injure a white runner while making a tag.

Several newspapers ran editorials blasting the IL and its white players for banning qualified black players from entering into the league and the abuse heaped upon the blacks who were already playing. *The Newark Call* wrote:

"If anywhere in the world the social barriers are broken down it is on the ball field. There many men of low birth and poor breeding are the idols of the rich and cultured; the best man is he who plays best. Even men of churlish disposition and coarse hues are tolerated on the field. In view of these facts the objection to colored men is ridiculous. If social distinctions are to be made, half the players in the country will be shut out.

Better the character and personal habits be the test. Weed out the toughs and intemperate men first, then it may be in order to draw the color line."

In the latter part of the nineteenth century, baseball was played by ordinary men, and the fans were mostly ordinary people who wanted to see a good game. Good breeding and social status weren't even a consideration. Ordinary whites didn't like the idea that blacks were their equals on or off the field.

Out of the Ballpark

THE first efforts to organize a black baseball league were unsuccessful. Walter Brown organized the League of Colored Baseball Clubs in 1887 with the purpose of preparing black players for acceptance into the majors. The opening game of the league was held May 6 in Pittsburgh. The fifteen hundred spectators were treated to a big parade before their hometown Keystones lost to the New York Gorhams, 11–8. It appeared as though the new black minor league was off to a good start, but to everybody's surprise it collapsed after three weeks due to financial problems. It would be many years before another all-black league would form.

Since the National League denied them a place in the sun and without a league of their own, all-black teams had only one recourse — barnstorm or apply for acceptance into the white minor and semipro leagues. During the 1880s and 1890s, there was less resistance to allowing all-black squads into the white minors than to integrated teams. So, during the last decades of the nineteenth century, several black teams were admitted to minor leagues.

Sol White was sixteen years old when the Walker brothers (Fleet and Weldy) were playing in the AA. He was so impressed with them that he began hanging around ball players, especially an amateur hometown team called the Bellaire Globes. He was offered a chance to play second base with the Globes. That was the beginning of Sol White's baseball career, which spanned almost four decades between 1887 and 1926.

During the 1880s, White saw the chances for black players diminishing, but he never wanted black players to give up their love of the sport. White played with the Cuban Giants, other semipro teams, and state leagues and was a field manager and a general manager for several all-black teams as well.

Although White was a good player, his greatest contribution was his writing. Much of what we know about these nineteenth-century black baseball clubs was written by Sol White in *The History of Colored Baseball* (1906). White said the Cuban Giants were the first professional black team. There are some who might disagree on that point, but very few will argue

The Cuban Giants in 1888.

that the Cuban Giants were the most flamboyant and the most popular all-black, professional team of their era. The team was organized in the summer of 1885, and by all accounts they were a showcase of late nineteenth-century black baseball.

Frank P. Thompson was the headwaiter at the Argyle Hotel, a Long Island resort for wealthy clients. In the evenings after work, he and a few of the other black employees formed a baseball team called the Babylon Athletics. They thrilled the guests by putting on exhibition games against local clubs. The team finished with a more than respectable record of six wins, two losses, and one tie. So, when the resort closed for the winter on October 1, the Athletics decided to stay together and barnstorm — which meant they traveled from city to city, playing local, semipro, and professional teams.

Sometimes they got to play exhibition games against major and minor league teams. As one barnstormer put it, "We played anybody, anywhere, for any amount."

The Athletics' road manager was John F. Lang, a wealthy white entrepreneur. A few weeks later, Lang had arranged for them to play an exhibition game against the seventh-place New York Metropolitans of the AA. The Babylon Athletics lost the game, 11–3, but gained valuable experience and respect.

Within the week, the team played and lost against the Philadelphia Athletics, 13–7. Philadelphia finished fourth in the AA that year. *The Sporting Life* commented that the Babylon Athletics lacked experience but could be a formidable opponent in the future.

Sol White told *Esquire* magazine in 1938, that it was about this time that the Babylon Athletics changed their name. Several of the men liked the New York Giants, so the Babylon Athletics became the Cuban Giants, although not one of them was a Cuban or could speak a word of Spanish. Many of the men were light-skinned blacks who could pass as Cubans. They spoke a made-up language to one another in an

An 1887 season ticket for the Cuban Giants.

effort to conceal their identities. Why did they want to be Cubans? Simple. Cubans were accepted in the major leagues, but blacks were not.

The Cuban Giants, now based in Trenton, New Jersey, became members of the Middle States League. They played white teams in and around Philadelphia, Harrisburg, Reading, and York. As predicted, they became strong competitors, beating the major league, Cincinnati Red Stockings in an exhibition game in 1887. They played the world-champion Detroit Tigers, but lost on a ninth-inning error, 6–4.

By 1888, the Cuban Giants were the most revered independent team in the country. The *Indianapolis Freeman* wrote:

"The Cuban Giants, the famous baseball club, have defeated the New Yorks, four games out of five, and are virtual champions of the world. The St. Louis Browns, Detroits, and Chicagos, afflicted with negrophobia are unable to bear the odium of being beaten by colored men, refused to accept the challenge."

Allowing for exaggeration, there are statistics that support the argument that the Cuban Giants were capable ball players equal to anyone playing at the time. They had the ability to become world champions if given a chance. George Williams, the Cuban Giants' star slugger, held a steady .391 career average. Arthur Thomas, his teammate, hit twenty-six doubles and ten triples, both league-leading totals. It wasn't surprising the Cuban Giants won their league pennant in 1890.

That same year, the league reorganized into the Eastern Interstate League, which folded in midseason, but not before it barred both black players and all-black teams from play. The Cuban Giants played one final season in the Connecticut State League and it disbanded. They went back to barnstorming, often playing amateur, semipro, and professional teams, and within a few years the team broke up.

The success of the Cuban Giants encouraged other teams to organize. Soon, all-black clubs were barnstorming all over the country. Many sprang up overnight and disappeared just as quickly. The Lincoln Giants from Nebraska and the Cuban X Giants from New York (they added the X to their names so as not to be confused with the Cuban Giants from Trenton) were excellent teams with strong players. With no league to represent them, these teams had no scheduled games. They played wherever they were invited. Each team was responsible for its own advertising. That's why they relied heavily upon showmanship to draw crowds. Parades, picnics, and fairs usually preceded most games.

In 1895, Bud Fowler organized the Page Fence Giants. When they arrived in town, the team rode

The Cuban X Giants played wherever they could.

Bud Fowler organized the Page Fence Giants in 1895.

bicycles down the street to advertise a game with either a hometown club or another barnstorming team. By 1899, Fowler had put together another squad called the All-American Black Tourists. They arrived wearing full dress suits, top hats, and silk umbrellas. In spite of what they had to do to draw a crowd, the players on these teams were excellent athletes. Contrary to the way they were portrayed in newspapers and journals, black players were not clowns or mediocre competitors. They were as good as any playing the game at the time. What they were doing was making the most out of a bad situation.

Blacks were also being locked out of other sports in which they had excelled, such as horse racing and boxing. Until the late 1890s most jockeys had been blacks.

Maybe one of the most surprising events in early baseball was the exclusion of black teams from the Ohio State League. Ohio had been a leading abolition state, known for its integrated colleges. "How could Ohio tolerate such an overt act of racism?" Weldy Walker asked when he wrote to league president W. H. McDermitt.

"The law is a disgrace to the present age," Walker

wrote. "There should be a broader cause — such as lack of ability, behavior, and intelligence — for barring a player rather than color."

Weldy Walker's letter was never answered, and the doors to the minor league teams were closing rapidly.

Bert Jones, pitcher and outfielder in the Kansas State League, played until 1898. He is believed to be one of the last blacks, along with Ben Wakefield, to play on an integrated minor league team.

Fleet Walker was so embittered by his experiences in baseball that he advocated the separation of the races. Walker, who was a successful writer and businessman, used his influence to promote the idea that the best chance for black survival was their return to Africa.

A few people, like Sol White, still held on to the hope that one day organized baseball would accept black players. He wrote:

"Baseball is a legitimate profession. It should be taken seriously by the colored player. An honest effort of his great ability will open the avenue in the near future wherein he may walk hand in hand with the opposite race in the greatest of all American games — baseball."

But the season for that vision was far in the future. By the end of the nineteenth century, blacks had lost more than just the right to play sports. In many southern states, blacks had lost the right to vote. Lynchings were commonplace. Black homes, businesses, and schools were being burned. Jim Crow laws humiliated black citizens who were forced to ride on segregated streetcars and trains. When these civil rights violations were challenged by blacks, the Supreme Court, in 1896, handed down its infamous *Plessy* v. *Ferguson* decision, upholding segregation and supporting the "separate but equal" doctrine, stemming from a lawsuit brought against a Louisiana railroad by Homer Plessy, a black man who had been forced to ride in a segregated car. Justice John Harlan, who cast the only dissenting vote on the court, wrote:

> *"I am of the opinion that the statute of Louisiana is inconsistent with the personal liberty of citizens, white and black, in that state, and hostile to both the spirit and the letter of the Constitution of the United States. . . ."*

The court's decision legalized racism and made it an acceptable American institution until 1954 when the Supreme Court reversed the 1896 decision in the famous *Brown* v. *Board of Education* case. During that time, the nation was divided along racial lines, but nowhere was that line drawn more clearly than in America's favorite sport — baseball!

CHAPTER

3

Batter Up!

BY 1900, most black players and teams — except for a few isolated instances — had been pushed to the sidelines where they watched helplessly as baseball developed without them. In the majors, the American League (AL) was struggling for recognition. The AL picked up four teams that the National League had just dropped and gained support from several splinter organizations, which included the Western League based in the Midwest. There was a costly and bitter league war between the NL and AL, but in 1903 a peace was negotiated and the dual major league structure we recognize today came into being.

Since neither the AL nor the NL accepted black players, what black baseball needed was a league, too, and a person strong-willed enough to manage a wide assortment of unique individuals. The person who accepted that challenge was Rube Foster, often called the "Father of the Negro Leagues."

Andrew "Rube" Foster understood baseball from the field to the management office, because he had been both a player and manager. During the first decade of the twentieth century, Rube had made his reputation pitching with the Chicago Leland Giants, named after the owner Frank Leland. Often black players were nicknamed after their white counterparts. Foster was dubbed "Rube" from Hall of Famer Rube Waddell, whom he outpitched in an exhibition game. When Rube was on the mound in Chicago, the Leland Giants were assured of a crowd.

In 1908, the Leland Giants and Mike Donlin's All-Stars had a six-game exhibition series. Donlin was a white major-leaguer who had formed a team made up of former big league players. The *Indianapolis Freeman* described the excitement that filled the air.

"For weeks the colored population of Chicago have been saving their money to go to the great series between their favorites and the All-Stars. A large amount of money was up between the two teams, and there was intense rivalry between the two aggregations."

Foster waited until his team was on the field, then he trotted to the mound as was his custom. The crowd went wild, cheering, chanting his name over and over. He dominated the day and won the game, 3–1.

The Leland Giants became the Chicago Giants, and Foster continued to pitch and manage the reorganized team.

For the next ten years, he and the Giants racked up one win after another. Foster never experienced "failure," but he didn't feel successful either. Black baseball lacked credibility, respectability, and reliability. No matter how many games black teams won against whites, they were still considered less capable. Barnstorming diverted players' attentions from the game with clownish antics that didn't do much for their image either. Players had no contracts, so their loyalty was fleeting. Whoever offered the most money, got the player, so pirating was commonplace and often destroyed well-established clubs.

Foster believed that if black players could prove themselves athletically capable and financially responsible, then white teams would eventually have to accept them in the majors. Until that time, he felt blacks had to organize and prove themselves.

Foster's attitude was based on the counsel of Booker T. Washington, a prominent black leader, who advocated gradualism with regard to integration. "In all things purely social we can be as separate as the fingers, yet one as the hand in all things essential to mutual progress."

Whites definitely agreed with Washington, because

Rube Foster (above right) first made his name pitching for the
Chicago Giants.

he seemingly accepted segregation. They used his
statement to build their case for the further denial of
basic human rights, in general, and white baseball
officials used Washington's philosophy to put an end
to black petitions for entry into the major leagues.

BASE BALL!!
FEDERAL LEAGUE PARK
SEPTEMBER 24-5-6
ORIGINAL A. B. C.'s
VS.
WORLD'S ALL NATIONS

**Heralding the First Appearance of The World's All Nations
The Great Donaldson will Positively Pitch 1 of These Games**

Composed of Hawaiians, Japanese, Cubans, Filipinos, Indians,
Chinese, direct from their native countries

JOHN DONALDSON
The Greatest Colored Pitcher in the World. Donaldson pitched 65 games last season, winning 60 of them.

JOSE MENDEZ
The Crack Cuban Pitcher, who defeated the Detroit Tigers, "American League Champions," 1-0, 10 innings, fanning Ty Cobb and Sam Crawford.

BLUKOI---The Giant Hawaiian, considered by critics to be the best 2nd baseman outside of Organized Base Ball.

PRIETO---The Sensational Cuban Pitcher, who won every game he pitched at Havana, Cuba, in 1915.

Traveling in Their Own Private Hotel Car
WILKINSON & GAUL, Sole Owners

Baseball drew its crowds from handbills like this one.

"One of these days," they promised. "When you're *ready*."

On the surface it might seem strange that Foster would agree with Washington's position. But Foster and black ball club owners believed that if black players were ever going to play, they had to organize themselves.

Foster proposed a separate professional major league for blacks. "In keeping with the times," he said, "I intend to do something concrete . . . for the race."

In 1920, an article in the *Chicago Defender* featured a story about Rube Foster. In it, he suggested that there be an association for black teams patterned after the major leagues. One league would be based in the Midwest and feature cities like Chicago, St. Louis, and Kansas City. The other league would be based in the East, covering New York, Philadelphia, and Pittsburgh.

The teams' owners didn't share Foster's vision. He was well respected, but they were suspicious and questioned how a league would benefit them. Two other attempts had been made to form a league, but each had failed. In 1906, the International League of Independent Baseball Clubs folded at the end of one season. And, in 1910, Beauregard Moseley, secretary of the Leland Giants, tried to form a National Negro Baseball League. It didn't hold together long enough to play a single game. Naturally, the owners weren't enthusiastic about another failed venture.

But Foster was persistent and on February 14, 1920, he and the owners of several top black teams met for a two-day conference at the YMCA in Kansas City. They discussed issues and concerns, smoothed ruffled feathers, eased tensions, and dispelled all rumors. The result was the formation of the Negro National League (NNL).

Foster and several other key players stayed up all night to work out a constitution for the new league. The next day, eight team owners put up five hundred dollars to bind themselves to the constitution. The owners named Foster president.

The first NNL featured eight teams: the Chicago Giants, the American Giants (also from Chicago), the St. Louis Giants, the Detroit Stars, the Indianapolis ABC's, the Cuban Stars from New York, the Dayton Marcos, and the Kansas City Monarchs.

At first, Foster wanted the teams and the league to be controlled exclusively by blacks. He wanted to veto the Monarchs' admission to the NNL, because J. L. Wilkinson, the owner, was white. But Wilkinson was well respected among players and owners, so Foster changed his mind. Later, Wilkinson became secretary of the NNL, and he and Foster formed a strong partnership.

Foster knew what had caused the other leagues to fold, so he learned by their mistakes and quickly made adjustments to offset those problems.

The first thing he did was to shift players from team to team in order to balance the new league. If a team had a weak pitching staff and another had four superstars, Foster sent one of the four pitchers to the weaker team. The same applied to hitting and fielding positions. The owners grumbled, but he explained that if the teams were allowed to keep their lineup, the league might die in the first season. And all of them would be losers.

Foster wouldn't allow the league debut until each

The Kansas City Monarchs in 1920.

club had secured, through lease or ownership, a place to play. On May 2, 1920, the NNL opened in Indianapolis when the ABC's beat the Chicago Giants, 4–2.

Limping forward a game at a time, Foster shepherded the NNL through the first year. The rivalries between cities like St. Louis and Chicago, Indianapolis and Kansas City worked very well, drawing as many as ten thousand fans on a Sunday afternoon. Foster's club, the American Giants, won the pennant that year. Unfortunately, there were no final standings listed, and records, beyond wins and losses, were not accurately kept. Foster had his fair share of personality conflicts with owners and players, too, but by all accounts given, the NNL enjoyed a minor financial success that first year. The real miracle was that it survived at all.

There were still a lot of kinks to iron out. But the NNL had lasted longer than any other black professional baseball organization before it. Some historians believe the league survived because of the strength and determination of Rube Foster.

Bases Loaded

THE 1920 major league season began with the revelation that eight Chicago White Sox players had conspired with gamblers and thrown the 1919 World Series against the Cincinnati Reds. Other players and teams were implicated, which resulted in further trials and suspensions. The much publicized scandal broke the trust with the public, which meant that baseball had to regain the confidence of the fans again. The big leagues entered the 1920s needing a morale booster, and they found him — Babe Ruth.

Although black baseball was scandal-free, it was not free of other problems. Teams were dogged by financial woes, poor media coverage, and unstable lineups. Black baseball needed help, too. The solutions to their problems could not be solved on the strength of one personality like the Babe.

At the beginning of the 1921 season, the primary concern of the NNL was stadiums. Owners of stadiums were charging black teams higher rents, insisting upon unreasonable leases or selling prices, and limiting playing time. The black Kansas City, Indianapolis, and Columbus teams could use stadiums in their cities only when they weren't in use — which was mostly on Sundays. Some of the cities were legalizing Sunday games, which really cut into NNL playing time, and made it very difficult for the NNL scheduler.

St. Louis and Detroit had very good contracts with the owners of their parks, but the other teams were experiencing difficulties. Even Foster's Giants ran into trouble, because while they owned their own portable bleachers, they didn't own the park they played in. During the second season, the Cuban Stars and Chicago Giants were forced to be "road" clubs, which meant essentially, all their scheduled games were "away games."

Some progress, however, was being made. In 1921, the Stars signed a lease with the Cincinnati Reds to use their stadium for four thousand dollars for the season. It was the first time a black baseball team had signed a lease to use a major league stadium regularly. To make sure they got their money, the Reds took twenty percent of the Stars' gate receipts until their lease was paid off.

No matter how tough times were within the NNL, Foster insisted that the NNL should always look as professional as possible. Everyone associated with the league was expected to be well polished on and off the field. No more parades and clown acts before a game.

Foster used his team, the Chicago American Giants, as a model for others to follow. The Giants traveled in style and comfort in a private Pullman train car. At that time a private car — especially a Pullman — was the pinnacle of luxury travel accommodations.

Dave Marlarcher, a former Giant and writer, enjoyed telling this story about the Giants' special traveling car.

"One day a white workman saw all of the black team members getting off, including Rube Foster. 'Hey there, hey there,' the man called, 'What are all you Negroes getting out of Mr. Rube Foster's car?' He had heard about Rube Foster being a great promoter and a great baseball man, but he didn't know Rube was a Negro. And you know what Rube said? 'I just happen to be Mr. Rube Foster.' You could have pushed that man over with a feather!"

Foster wasn't just interested in style. He tried to put substance into the league as well. Some of the NNL teams were unstable and that weakened the whole

Dave Malarcher played with Rube Foster's Chicago
American Giants.

league. When necessary, Rube used his own money to get teams home and often paid players' salaries. Still, some of the teams were too weak to hold on.

The Dayton Marcos dropped out midseason and was replaced by the Columbus Buckeyes, who lasted until the end of the 1921 season. The Buckeyes came back in the mid-1920s and remained a viable team until the 1940s. Several other teams dropped out because they couldn't hold on financially. "He [Foster] just wouldn't give up," Marlarcher wrote in an article. "The success of the league meant everything to him."

There was a growing resentment among the owners and baseball watchers toward Foster. While serving as the president of the NNL, he was also the league's booking agent. He hired all the umpires, yet he was a club owner. Foster also netted $11,220 in 1920 just for booking fees. Actually Foster hadn't done anything illegal and he put most of the money back into league operations, but that didn't seem to matter. Criticism mounted.

Players also accused Foster of choosing umpires who were partial to his Giants. Foster answered by calling them whiners and spoilers. The debate became an all-out quarrel, and Foster was not one to back down. He wasn't going to give up one iota of power.

While Foster was battling to stay in control of the NNL, teams in the South and on the East Coast decided to sidestep Foster and the NNL and start leagues of their own.

A group of southern baseball owners had organized the Negro Southern League a few months after the NNL was formed. Although the teams varied from year to year, Atlanta, New Orleans, Birmingham, Nashville, Jacksonville, Montgomery, and Memphis consistently fielded teams. But there was bad blood between the Negro Southern League and the NNL.

The Negro Southern League was considered a minor league to the northern teams. Since no formal contract or agreement existed between the two, the NNL often took ball players from the Negro Southern League without compensation to the owners.

Other black minor and semipro leagues began forming, too, but none of them seriously offered a challenge to the NNL. By far the NNL had the recognition and the reputation. Then on December 16, 1923, five eastern clubs met in Philadelphia and organized the Eastern Colored League. The league teams included the Brooklyn Royal Giants, Lincoln Giants of New York, the Bacharach Giants of Atlantic City, the Baltimore Black Sox, and the Hilldale Club of Darby, Pennsylvania.

This league had no elected president, but there was a five-man board of commissioners made up of the owners of the teams. But everybody knew the leader of the Eastern League was Nat C. Strong, owner of the Brooklyn Royal Giants. He served as the new league's booking agent, which was a powerful posi-

The Brooklyn Royal Giants, above in 1915, joined the Eastern Colored League in 1923.

tion. Strong and Foster were equally matched for the battle that was to come.

The Eastern Colored League had a decisive advantage over the NNL. The 1920s were an exciting time for African Americans in the East, especially in New York where blacks were experiencing a time of growth and self-awareness. Historian Lerone Bennett describes the period known as the "Negro Renaissance"

Three women on Seventh Avenue in Harlem in 1927.

as a "period of extraordinary activity on the part of the black artists and extraordinary receptivity on the part of the white public, [which] reached a peak in the 1920s." All over the country, black artists made outstanding contributions to American literature, art, music, drama, dance, education, and sports. One of the best-known members of the renaissance elite was the literary giant Langston Hughes, who wrote *The Weary Blues* in 1926. The 1920s also produced several significant political leaders like Marcus Garvey, who inspired many followers to return to Africa, and A. Philip Randolph, who helped start the Brotherhood of Sleeping Car Porters in 1926.

"Up East" was where the action was, and everybody wanted to go there, especially Harlem. The Department of Labor reported in 1923 that five hundred thousand blacks had left the South in the preceding year. Wealthy whites were more willing to invest in black endeavors and attend black functions. So the Eastern Colored League drew both black and white crowds. Also, Strong was able to attract some of the better players who liked the idea of living and playing in exciting cities like New York and Philadelphia. Even so, the Eastern Colored League was burdened with many of the same problems that the NNL suffered.

In 1924, Foster tried to negotiate a merger between the NNL and the Eastern Colored League. But neither manager was willing to give up his powerful position. That ignited a league war that almost destroyed the NNL. Strong lured ten members of the Indianapolis ABC's to the Eastern Colored League. The ABC's had

BOLDEN   SANTOP   WINTERS   CURRIE   LEE   CARR   C.JOHNSON   J.JOHNSON   RYAN

The Hilldale Club of Kansas in the first Negro World Series in 1927.

been weakened by the death of their manager, C. I. Taylor, in 1922. Taylor had been the backbone of the club. After his death and the Eastern raid, the ABC's folded in 1924. Foster replaced them with the Memphis Red Sox, the second southern team to join the NNL.

Since they couldn't combine the clubs, Foster and Strong agreed to have a series at the end of the 1924 season. The leagues' two pennant winners would face each other in a "Negro Leagues World Series." The NNL champions, the Kansas City Monarchs, met the Hilldale Club, champions of the East. Kansas City beat Hilldale in a hard-fought series and won their

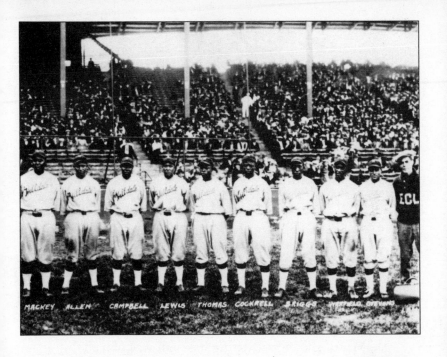

MACKEY ALLEN CAMPBELL LEWIS THOMAS COCKRELL BRIGGS WINFIELD STEVENS

first world championship. The games were very well attended by large and enthusiastic crowds.

These games helped showcase some of black baseball's best talent. Although Babe Ruth dominated the sports pages, African Americans had their heroes, too: outfielders Oscar Charleston and James Thomas "Cool Papa" Bell, third baseman William Julius "Judy" Johnson, shortstop John Beckwith, second baseman Newt Allen, first baseman George "Mule" Suttles, catcher George "Chappie" Johnson, and pitchers Wilber "Bullet" Rogan and left-handed Andy "Lefty" Cooper.

CHAPTER

5

The Lineup

SOME of the most exciting baseball was played during the 1920s by black players who put in performances that were second to none. Some of them were college-trained athletes. Others honed their skills playing for military teams or in foreign leagues, and more than a few learned how to throw, hit, and run in ghetto alleys or reform schools. Although they came from different social and economic backgrounds, they didn't let that stop them from playing together.

Celebrities and political leaders flocked to see the baseball heroes of the day. Charlie Biot of the New York Black Yankees remembered: "Everybody got dressed to the nines to go to the ball game, not like today, when people dress like they're going to rake leaves."

Memorable players from the 1920s gave fans their quarter's worth, from New York to Chicago and from Kansas City to Birmingham.

The pitchers in the 1920s were showmen as well as athletes, and the fans loved to watch them deliver balls that zinged and zipped and dipped and curved. Walter Johnson and "Smoky" Joe Williams had fastballs that held impressive records until Richard "Cannonball" Dick Redding·came along. He was known for his hesitation pitch and fastball. Rumor was that Cannonball had helped Hall of Fame slugger Lou Gehrig hit fastballs. Gehrig, of course, went to the New York Yankees and made baseball history.

John Donaldson had a sharp-breaking curveball that moved with the speed of a fastball. Counted among the best to stand on the mound in the Negro Leagues, Donaldson began his career in professional baseball in 1912 with the Tennessee Rats, a barnstorming team that entertained as well as competed on the diamond. While pitching for J. L. Wilkinson's All-Nations Team just before World War I, Donaldson hurled three successive no-hitters. Wilkinson, who also owned the Kansas City Monarchs, said Cannonball Donaldson was the most amazing pitcher he had ever seen.

During the early 1920s, when Donaldson was at his peak, he hurled for teams in the NNL and the Eastern Colored League.

There was a story circulating that a minor league coach had offered Donaldson ten thousand dollars to move to Cuba, change his name, then return some months later as a Cuban. That way the coach could sign Donaldson without a problem. But Donaldson, no doubt, remembered the incident involving Charlie Grant.

Most major league owners and managers didn't care about what color the player was, just so long as he could help the team win. But white players and fans did care. To get around the lockout of blacks, some managers devised schemes that resembled a carnival sideshow.

John J. McGraw was the manager of the Baltimore Orioles. During the 1901 spring training session, McGraw saw Charlie Grant play an exhibition game. McGraw wanted to sign him badly, but how could he get around the color barrier? He decided to pass Grant off as a Native American — a Cherokee, whose name was Tokohama (the name of a river that McGraw had found on a map). Grant was willing to do anything to get a chance to play in the majors, so he went along with the deception by dressing up in a stereotypical native costume and painting his face. The whole disguise was an insult to the Cherokee nation for it wasn't remotely authentic. For a while, the sham worked, but a few white players recognized Grant even with the disguise, and though McGraw and Grant protested loudly that he was a "full-blooded

Charlie Grant disguised himself as a Native American in order to play briefly in the major leagues.

Indian," the ruse was uncovered. Grant, known for-ever after as "Chief," never played in a regular season major league game. He returned to the Columbia Giants in the NNL where he played until his death in 1932.

Cannonball Donaldson decided the offer to play in the majors came at too high a price. He sent a message that he wasn't willing to become a Cuban just to play in the majors. If they couldn't sign him as an African American, then he wasn't interested.

Oddly enough, José "Joe" Mendez actually *was* a Cuban, but he had dark skin, so he was locked out of the majors, too. Mendez pitched for Foster's American Giants, the Detroit Stars, and the Kansas City Monarchs. He died in Havana in 1928.

Another star hurler was Wilber "Bullet" Rogan. They called him Bullet because he could zip a ball past a batter at bullet speed.

Between 1911 and 1919, Rogan served several hitches in the military. For a while, he played baseball for the 25th Infantry, stationed in Hawaii, and the Los Angeles White Sox while he was a civilian. During the 1920s, the big six-footer came back to the Midwest and pitched for the Kansas City Monarchs, averaging about thirty games a year.

During the 1920s there were more ball players than there were clubs to support them, but there was always need for strong catchers. George "Chappie" Johnson caught for the Chicago Giants and the St. Louis Giants in the NNL and the Philadelphia Royal Stars in the Eastern Colored League.

Chappie Johnson took the initiative and organized several baseball teams in upstate New York, and in 1928 he came to New York and organized the Chappie Johnson All-Stars and barnstormed in Montreal.

Frank "Pete" Duncan, Jr., a native of Kansas City, spent most of his career catching for the Kansas City Monarchs. He joined them in 1922 and stayed on until the 1940s. One of the highest-paid players in the Eastern Colored League was said to be Louis "Top" Santop (Loftin). As catcher for the Hilldale Club and a strong hitter, he reportedly made five hundred dollars a month, a fabulous salary in the 1920s, considering bacon and eggs cost twenty cents in a restaurant.

Benjamin "Ben" Taylor, George "Mule" Suttles, and Newt Allen made their reputations playing the bases and swatting balls out of the ballpark. Shortstop John Beckwith of the Chicago Giants, at the age of nineteen, smacked a ball over the left-field fence at Redland Field in Cincinnati. He was the first to do it — white or black. During his best years (1927 and 1928), Beckwith hit a total of 126 home runs! Another powerful bat was shortstop Richard "Dick" Lundy, a switch-hitter who held a steady .300 average throughout his career.

Right behind Lundy was shortstop Willie Wells whose career began in 1923 with a San Antonio semi-pro team. They called him "the Devil" because his bat was "red-hot." The following year he was in St. Louis with the Giants, then on to the Stars. Wells, too, maintained a .300 or better batting average.

Infielder William Julius "Judy" Johnson *was* the Hilldale team in the 1920s. During the first Negro

World Series of 1924, Johnson led Hilldale's hitters
with a .341 series average.

David Malarcher was a hard-hitting, intelligent infielder. Known as "Gentleman Dave" because of his
genteel southern style, Malarcher played third base
for the Chicago American Giants. He may have been
a gentleman, but he was a fierce competitor who followed Rube Foster as the manager of the American
Giants, a team that dominated the NNL in the early
1920s.

Several excellent outfielders during the 1920s were
Spotswood "Spots" Poles, James "Jimmie" Lyons,
and Chaney White. Sports heroes are usually presented larger than life, but Caribbean star Martin Dihigo and Oscar Charleston and James Thomas "Cool
Papa" Bell were legends even then.

It was said that Oscar Charleston was "fast enough
to stand behind second base and outrun the longest
line drive, powerful enough to loosen a ball's cover
with one hand, fearless enough to snatch the hood off
a Ku Klux Klansman."

Charleston, born in 1896, learned how to be tough
growing up in a rough neighborhood in Indianapolis.
He and his brother fought their way to and from
school. His brother became a professional boxer, and
Oscar, at age fifteen, joined the Army. While serving
in the all-black 24th Infantry Regiment in the Phil-
ippines, he became a star player on the regimental
baseball and track teams.

Oscar Charleston played for the Homestead Grays.

After he was discharged, Charleston returned to Indianapolis and signed up with the ABC's. He was an ideal player, who could play several positions well, but he had the speed and agility needed to be a formidable outfielder. At the bat, he had the strength to slam balls out of the park and the speed to turn a single into a double.

In 1924, Charleston was one of the players who left the ABC's for greener pastures with the Hilldale Club of the Eastern Colored League. His absence was sorely felt by the ABC's, because Charleston was, without exception, one of the finest all-around players in baseball.

He was often compared to the legendary Ty Cobb — the first person elected to the Hall of Fame — in style and personality. Both were fierce competitors whose tempers sometimes got them into trouble on and off the field. Bobby White, a former teammate of Charleston's, explained: "[Charleston] was all business — the business of baseball, and this made him seem short-tempered and mean." White remembered him as a warm and friendly man who liked "to kid around." Although there were people who differed with White's assessment of Charleston, most of his teammates liked and respected him. And his fans adored him. The *Pittsburgh Courier* wrote: "Scores of school kids turned out regularly just to see Oscar perform. He was to them what Babe Ruth is to kids of a lighter hue."

James Thomas "Cool Papa" Bell played well into the 1940s but was in peak form during the 1920s. Satchel Paige said Bell could "pull the light switch and run across the room, hop in bed, and cover up before the light went out." Some historians say Bell was the fastest runner who ever stole a base, including Ty Cobb. Since there are no records to support that assertion, the best that can be said is Bell was *one of* the fastest runners in the 1920s.

One of Cool Papa's former teammates said, "When Bell hit a ball back to the pitcher, the fans would yell, 'Hurry!'" And, Judy Johnson told a reporter that when "Bell was at bat with no one on base, the infielders moved in as if a man were on third with one out. You couldn't play back in your regular position or you'd never throw him out."

Bell left Mississippi in 1920 at the age of seventeen. His first stop was St. Louis, where he, along with four of his brothers, played for an amateur team, the Compton Hill Cubs. By 1922, he was in East St. Louis, Illinois, playing semipro ball, but by the end of the year he'd been picked up by the St. Louis Stars. Like most players during that period, Bell played a number of positions before he finally ended up in the outfield.

James Bell got his nickname when he was a nineteen-year-old pitcher for the Stars. He was young, but he stayed composed and struck out Oscar Charleston. His teammates started calling him "Cool." Bill Gatewood, the manager, added the "Papa."

What Cool Papa Bell lacked in power, he made up for in speed. Fans loved it when he turned singles into doubles or sometimes triples. William "Yank" Yancey, who played for a number of teams including the Philadelphia Stars from 1923–1936, told this story about Bell. "I haven't seen anybody yet could run with Cool. When I was on the Lincoln Giants, we played in a little park in New York called the Catholic Protectory up in the Bronx. That was our regular home field." Judy Johnson had told him how fast Cool Papa Bell was. Yancey said:

"Now, I could throw, so I said nobody can outrun a baseball. So the first time Cool Papa came to New York with the St. Louis Stars, he hit a ball into right field. Chino Smith was out there, and he could field a ball, and if you made a wide turn at first base he could throw you out trying to hustle back. I went out to get the throw, and when I looked up Cool Papa was slowing up going into third! And I said to myself, That sonofagun didn't touch second. *Next time up, he hit another one about the same place. Now nobody got a three-base hit in that little park. I don't care where they hit the ball. And I watched this guy run. Well, he came across second base and it looked like his feet weren't touching the ground!"*

The great "Cool Papa" Bell was famous for his speed when stealing bases.

Stories like Yancey's are commonplace among players who saw Cool Papa Bell run. Although Bell spent four years playing in Mexico where life was less restrictive, he still played long enough and well enough in the States to be inducted into Baseball's Hall of Fame.

Like Cool Papa Bell, Hall of Famer Martin Dihigo was a legend in his own time, too. Born in 1905, the

The Cuban player, Martin Dihigo, also played in America.

Cuban superstar came to the United States hoping for a chance in the majors. In the early 1920s, several light-skinned Cubans had been signed with the National and American Leagues, so African-American players watched with interest, hoping that if darker Cubans were accepted in the majors, then maybe they would be next. But once again, hopes were shattered. Neither Mendez nor Dihigo — two of the best coming out of Cuba — got offers, simply because their skin color was too dark.

Dihigo spent part of his long and illustrious career playing in Cuba and part of the time in the United States with the New York Cubans made up of dark-skinned Caribbean players.

During a career that lasted well over the age of forty, Dihigo presented a triple threat every time he took the field. He could pitch, field, and bat, and all with lethal precision. And, when he wasn't playing, he managed the team. "He was a tough guy to beat," remembered players like Page and Leonard who played with and against him in several East-West All-Star Games. "Dihigo could have played with the best among them," said Satchel Paige.

CHAPTER

6

You're Out!

RUBE Foster was hospitalized in 1926, the same year that the NNL American Giants beat the Eastern Colored League Bacharachs in the Negro World Series. As Foster's health began to deteriorate, so did the NNL. When he died in an Illinois mental hospital on December 9, 1930, three thousand mourners — blacks and whites, rich and poor — attended his funeral.

By then, the Eastern Colored League was already dead and two years later the NNL collapsed. The Negro Southern League (now considered a major league) was just barely hanging on. Foster's team was taken over by businessman Robert Cole and the name was changed to Cole's American Giants. Some of the NNL teams joined the Negro Southern League.

In 1930, during the Depression, there were millions of people out of work. Blacks, who are most often the last hired and first fired, felt the sting of the Depression earlier and endured it longer. Black baseball was no different. While major league baseball was extremely hard hit by the Depression, black baseball was practically destroyed. Attendance, which was never really that high for NNL games, dropped sharply, because African Americans didn't have jobs. People were concerned about food, clothing, and shelter. Going to a baseball game was not a priority.

So, the early 1930s were a test of survival, and the teams that made it through those tough years were those who found new ways to raise attendance — which meant higher revenues.

J. L. Wilkinson's Kansas City Monarchs had been one of the strongest teams in the NNL. They had a large following in Kansas City, but not enough to keep the team afloat. Wilkinson had a portable generator and lights designed, which made it possible to play night games. It was a novelty and people came to a game or two out of curiosity. It would be several years before the first night game would be played in the major leagues. Wilkinson instituted "ladies' day," "family day," and "two-for-the-price-of-one specials" to bring in the fans, but Wilkinson wasn't able to keep the revenues high enough to meet expenses. He decided to take the team on the road, barnstorming across America, playing anywhere it could. It was the right decision, because the Monarchs were one of the teams that survived the 1930–1932 seasons, the toughest in the history of baseball.

The Cuban Stars, the Cleveland Cubs, the St. Louis Stars, the Chicago American Giants, the reorganized Indianapolis ABC's, and the Louisville White Sox continued to compete, but they were forced to barnstorm during the 1931 season. There were so few games played that year, no final standings were published, but the St. Louis Stars were declared league winners.

The cities were hit hard by the Depression, so some of the teams barnstormed in rural areas and returned to "clowning" routines where the rules of baseball were sacrificed for the sake of entertainment — some of it demeaning. The Tennessee Rats, the Ethiopians, and the Zulu Cannibals were three clubs that thrived on their comic revues before, during, and after their games. Rube Foster had worked so hard to rid black baseball of that image. Sportswriter Wendell Smith echoed Foster's warning that these kind of performances only reinforced black stereotypes. "Negroes must realize the danger in insisting that black ball players paint their faces and go through minstrel show revues before each ball game." At the time, however, the clown teams were packing fans in, so many of the managers thought survival was more important than image.

Even traditional teams like the Kansas City Monarchs, the Chicago Giants, and the Detroit Stars, relented a little. They took the winning combination of good sportsmanship and showmanship to people in small midwestern and southern towns who ordinarily didn't get to see the quality of baseball delivered by players such as Cool Papa Bell, Oscar Charleston, and Judy Johnson. In this way, some of the best of the first Negro League teams made it through the 1932 season.

Franklin Delano Roosevelt was elected president in November 1932. He and his administration immediately set up government programs that put people back to work, and for the first time in many years, a

The Kansas City Monarchs seen in front of their bus with their owner, J. L. Wilkinson.

Third baseman William Julius "Judy" Johnson.

president and first lady were showing concern about the African-American population. People were hopeful and they expressed it by returning to the ballparks to cheer for their favorite teams. So, as the country limped toward economic recovery, so did baseball.

Some of the Negro Leagues' clubs hadn't been able to hold on and had disappeared from the scene; some had reorganized under new owners, moved to another city, or merged with another team. The Kansas City Monarchs were still around, so were the Chicago Giants, and the Indianapolis ABC's. But then, some new teams had emerged.

Two teams that kept black baseball alive and well in the thirties were the Posey Brothers' Homestead Grays and William Augustus "Gus" Greenlee's Crawford Colored Giants.

Franklin D. Roosevelt shaking hands with admirers.

Cumberland "Cum" Posey was the ambitious and talented manager of the Homestead Grays, located a few miles southwest of Pittsburgh. Seeward "See" Posey was the co-owner of the club and business manager. Cum Posey knew the importance of having a strong league, so his idea was to reorganize the Eastern Colored League. In 1932, he organized the East-West League, but it didn't survive the summer, and the Grays went back to barnstorming.

The next year, an unlikely character made a lasting impact on black baseball. He was Gus Greenlee, a Pittsburgh restaurant-tavern owner and numbers racketeer. Today people buy lottery tickets, hoping to get rich instantly. Several decades ago people "played the numbers," which was an illegal form of gambling. They placed a bet on a combination of three numbers, for example, 345, 756, 912, or any of the infinite possibilities. The number for the day was based on a formula derived from stock market figures. Greenlee controlled the numbers racket in Pittsburgh, which supplied him with an inexhaustible source of money, and he spent it lavishly on his ball club and even built them their own stadium to play in. Although he had no prior experience in baseball, either as a manager or player, he had, by 1931, raided Poseys' Grays and assembled one of the most powerful teams in Negro League history — the Crawfords. Greenlee knew that the clubs that owned their own parks were better off than renters and barnstormers. So it was a sound in-

"Cum" Posey (far right, wearing tie and cap) with the
Homestead Grays.

vestment to build a stadium. Gus Greenlee's field
opened on April 29, 1932, to a packed house. Greenlee
lost sixteen thousand dollars during the first year, but
he didn't quit. In 1933, to protect his investment,
Greenlee reorganized the second Negro National
League, which lasted until 1948.

The newly organized NNL included teams from the
East and Midwest. Like Foster, Greenlee had total
control over the league, because he had the money
and power to keep it. His way was the only way. But
before long, old rivalries resurfaced, and, in 1937, the
Negro American League (NAL) was started by H. G.
Hall, a club owner with clubs in the Midwest and
South. The NNL was on an eastern circuit. Cum Posey's Homestead Grays were a charter club in the new

NNL, so that made Pittsburgh the capital of black baseball and the home of two powerhouse teams.

The Homestead Grays also played in the Gus Greenlee Stadium until 1937, when they moved to Washington and played in Griffith Stadium. By that time, Greenlee had put Posey out of the NNL, because he had stolen away some of the best Crawford players.

Greenlee's wasn't the first black ball club to own its stadium. The Hilldale Club, which had started in 1910 near Darby, Pennsylvania, incorporated in 1920, and used the stock proceeds to buy a field. It had a grandstand that could seat five thousand.

The Negro World Series that was so popular in the 1920s was overshadowed by the East-West Games of the 1930s. After the ANL was formed, the East squad came from the NNL, and the West players came from the NAL. Starting in 1933, it was played every year until the NNL folded in 1948. The idea for the game came from Roy Sparrow, one of Greenlee's employees. It was a production more than a game, which drew crowds of up to twenty thousand.

Characteristically, Greenlee handled all the promotion and took ten percent of the game receipts, until he was forced to resign the presidency of the NNL in 1939. The players were paid nothing extra for playing the game, but after they threatened a strike, they were paid one hundred to two hundred dollars out of the gate proceeds.

OSCAR CHARLESTON, Manager

WALTER CANNADY
† All-Round Player In Baseball

HARRY WILLIAMS
Catcher

W. G. PERKINS
Catcher

BOBBIE WILLIAMS
Third Base

CHESTER WILLIAMS
Shortstop

"JOSH" GIBSON
Hardest Hitter In Negro Baseball

SPEARMAN
Left Field

SAM STREETER
Ace Lefthander

ROY KINCANNON
Pitcher

TED RADCLIFF
Pitcher

ROY WILLIAMS
Pitcher

"SATCHELL" PAGE
Called the Speed Ball King

L. D. LIVINGSTON
Right Field

JIMMIE CRUTCHFIELD
Center Field

PITTSBURGH CRAWFORDS

BASEBALL CLUB, Inc.

PITTSBURGH'S COLORED CHAMPIONS

PLAYING IN THEIR OWN

NEW $100,000 GREENLEE FIELD

Pittsburgh,Pa.,June 6th,1932.

Lloyd P.Thompson,Secretary,
East-West Colored League,
Darby,Pa.

Dear Sir:

I beg to tender my sincere thanks for the care and consideration given my list of queries submitted at our last informal meeting,in Philadelphia.

If the East-West Organization is to endure, and enjoy a measure of growing popularity and prosperity,it must have a base four-square,and in its structure,retain only members,tranquil in the knowledge that their rules and laws assure mutual safety and the promise of a fair reward.

Permit me please,to take you back along the lane of memory;do you recall the rancor that existed in Organized Baseball,when Garry Hermann and Ban. Johnson,controlled the "National Commission";remember,if you will the scandal that developed during and after the 1919 World's Series;and how "Baseball" was only saved from destruction by the selection of Judge Landis as it's High Commissioner.

Did his HONOR,then,have an interest in any team,in either league,or has he since acquired one?

Would it not be well to select the "Czar" of your Organization from a source that would have no financial share,in any East-West League club?

Very truly yours,

Thos. J. Higgins.

A letter from Thomas Higgins of the Pittsburgh Crawfords.

"Stretching Buck" Leonard of the Homestead Grays.

At that time, some of black baseball's titans who
matched skills in the famous East-West Games included Oscar Charleston, Judy Johnson, Cool Papa
Bell, Ted Page, Leroy Matlock, Jimmie Crutchfield,
Buck Leonard, and the legendary Satchel Paige.

Black Diamonds

IN 1932, Gus Greenlee heard that a brilliant pitcher named Satchel Paige might be available. Paige accepted Greenlee's offer of two hundred fifty dollars a month and slipped comfortably into a Crawford uniform. Although Paige had been bumping around Negro League baseball diamonds most of his life, it was while pitching with the Pittsburgh Crawfords that his rise to fame began.

They nicknamed him "Satchel" because when he was a boy he carried people's luggage (satchels) at the Mobile, Alabama, train station. The lanky kid with long arms and very big feet carried so many at a time, some of his friends said he looked like a "Satchel Tree." The name stuck.

LeRoy "Satchel" Paige was born July 7, 1906, in

Mobile, Alabama, the same year sixty-two blacks were reported lynched in the United States. Growing up poor and under the cloud of segregation and discrimination, young Satchel wasn't a likely candidate for success. In fact he learned how to throw rocks with incredible accuracy, and his rock-throwing and the rough older boys he was hanging around with got him into trouble. While in reform school, he learned how to throw a baseball. By the time he was released in 1923, at seventeen, Satchel was good enough to play professional ball.

From 1926, when Satchel was in his twenties, he played with a number of teams — the Chattanooga Lookouts, the New Orleans Black Pelicans, the Baltimore Black Sox, the Birmingham Black Barons, and the Nashville Elite Giants — never committing himself to more than two or three seasons with any one club until 1932, when he joined the Pittsburgh Crawfords.

"Satchel loved to throw a baseball," said Josh Gibson, who was sometimes a teammate and sometimes an opponent. It didn't matter where or with what team — Satchel just loved to pitch.

There are many stories about Satchel's legendary pitches. He had names for all of them. His "two-hump blooper" was his change-up pitch. But his specialty was a fastball he called a "bee ball." According to Satchel, all a batter heard was the humming of the ball as it zinged over the plate.

Biz Mackey, who caught for Satchel, said:

*"When [the ball] is that fast . . . it tends to dis-
appear. Yes, disappear. I've heard about Satchel
throwing pitches that wasn't hit, but that never
showed up in the catcher's mitt nevertheless.
They say the catcher, the umpire, and the batboys
looked all over for that ball, but it was gone.
Now, how do you account for that?"*

Another of Satchel's amazing pitches was his "hesitation ball," delivered by planting his foot, halting in
midthrow, then releasing the ball.

In 1932, Satchel's incredible arm led the Pittsburgh
Crawfords to a 99–36 win-loss season record. His
personal stats were very impressive, too: twenty-three
victories and seven losses.

In 1934, Satchel asked Greenlee for a raise. Greenlee
made him an offer, but Satchel laughed and said, "I
wouldn't pitch ice cubes for that amount," and he
walked away from a two-year contract in midseason.
Greenlee was furious and had Paige banned from the
NNL for all of 1935.

Satchel never missed a step. He spent most of his
time barnstorming and playing exhibition games
against All-Star teams formed by white players such
as Dizzy Dean and Babe Ruth. It was easy for him to
put a team together, because exhibition games against
major-leaguers were important to black players because they got coverage in the white press and it also
helped to settle disputes about blacks' abilities on the

diamond. Most of the white major-leaguers who faced Satchel walked away saying he was the best. "If only you were white," Satchel often heard.

In one of those All-Star games, Satchel was matched against major league hurler Dizzy Dean. The score was 0–0 at the bottom of the ninth. As Paige approached the mound for the tenth inning, he met Dean coming off the field. "I don't know what you're going to do, Mr. Dean," Satchel drawled in his deep southern accent, "but I'm not going to give up any runs if we have to stay here all night." And he didn't. Satchel won the game when his team scored a run off Dean in the fourteenth inning.

Dean was heard later to say, "Satchel and me would be worth a quarter of a million to any major league club. We'd clinch the pennant mathematically by the Fourth of July and go fishin' until the World Series. Between us we'd win sixty games."

"Heck," responded Satchel when he heard what Dean had said, "maybe I'd win all sixty by myself."

In another exhibition game in 1935, Satchel pitched against Joe DiMaggio, who was being watched by the New York Yankees' scouts. DiMaggio on his fourth time at bat hit a single in the tenth inning, and the scout rushed to send a telegram: "DiMaggio all we hoped he'd be; hit Satch one for four."

Satchel played for Greenlee during the 1936 season, but by 1937, the renegade was off again, this

The legendary pitcher Satchel Paige.

time to the Dominican Republic. President Rafael L. Trujillo was assembling a team. Trujillo believed his reelection depended upon the results of a series played against his political rival's ball club, the Dragones. He reportedly paid Satchel thirty thousand dollars to build a winning team for him.

At about that time, Greenlee was having problems with his numbers operation. A police informant — a janitor — was reporting everything that was happening within Greenlee's organization to the vice squad. After several raids in which large amounts of money were confiscated, Greenlee began to feel the pinch. He announced that the players would have to pay their own expenses at spring training. Rumors spread like wildfire that Greenlee was broke. Knowing how unstable most black ball clubs were at the time, the players panicked.

Satchel seized the opportunity and recruited some of the Pittsburgh Crawfords to join him in the Dominican Republic. Nine top Crawfords, including Cool Papa Bell and Josh Gibson, took the offer. The team was named the Trujillo Stars. It didn't take long for them to realize that they *needed* to win. According to Paige and Bell, Trujillo's army kept the players under armed guard the whole time they played. "They don't kill people over baseball?" Cool Papa Bell asked. "Down here they do," someone answered.

Rudolfo Fernández, pitcher for the Dragones, said the stories about the importance of the games were greatly exaggerated. Either way, it doesn't seem there was much margin for error. The Trujillo Stars won the six-game series in Santo Domingo.

By 1938, Greenlee's situation was more stable, so the runaways came back to the Pittsburgh Crawfords and willingly accepted the fine of one week's salary. Greenlee sold Satchel to the Newark Eagles, but the nomad refused to settle down. He was off to Mexico. The NNL promptly banned Satchel "for life" this time.

Satchel played in the Mexican League, pitching all winter and well into the summer. He hurled every day, sometimes for a month without rest, so by the end of summer his arm was too sore to lift over his

The Dominican Republic Trujillo All Stars in 1937.

In 1938, Gus Greenlee had Satchel Paige banned from baseball.

head. Returning to the States, Satchel was told by a doctor that he'd never pitch again. It looked as though one of the greatest pitchers of all time was washed up at age thirty-two. The irony, of course, is that Satchel's story was just beginning.

One of the players who went with Satchel to the Dominican Republic was a powerful hitter named Josh Gibson. Whenever people gather to celebrate baseball's greatest sluggers, Gibson is sure to be mentioned right along with Babe Ruth. Some people who have carefully studied both players' lifetime performances believe that Gibson might have been better than Ruth. Without a doubt, however, Gibson's career statistics support the claim that he was one of the best batters ever.

Gibson and Ruth were contemporaries, but each had a different batting style. Ruth swung with his whole body, twisting like a human screw when he missed the ball. Gibson's power came from his upper body. Teammate Judy Johnson remembered Gibson:

"It was just a treat to watch him hit the ball. There was no effort at all. Gibson would just walk up there, and he would always turn his left sleeve up, and then just before he swung he'd lift that left foot up."

If the powerful right-hander connected with the ball, it was more often than not a home run.

As with Satchel Paige, stories about Gibson's powerful hitting are abounding. It is said Gibson hit a ball while playing a game in Pittsburgh so hard, so high, and so far, it vanished. The next day when he was playing in Philadelphia, a startled outfielder caught a ball that fell out of the sky unexplainably. The umpire, seeing what had happened, called Gibson out — "yesterday in Pittsburgh!"

The story is an exaggeration, but the facts about Josh Gibson are just as startling.

Gibson didn't learn how to play baseball until his family moved to Pittsburgh when he was twelve years old. He was born in a small town outside Atlanta,

Georgia, four days before Christmas 1911, the same year the National Association for the Advancement of Colored People was incorporated, on June 20, in New York. He was named Joshua after his grandfather. Fleeing the oppression of the rural South, the Gibson family moved to Pittsburgh in 1923.

Although he excelled in a number of sports, he enjoyed baseball the most. He made it through the ninth grade where he learned a trade, but his heart was in baseball. He played for a semipro team, and earned a reputation for being a good catcher but a better hitter.

On July 25, 1930, nineteen-year-old Gibson was in the grandstand of Forbes Field, watching the Kansas City Monarchs and the Homestead Grays battle it out. It was a night game and the Monarchs had brought along their portable lighting system. The Grays, who hadn't played under the lights before, had to change their pitching signals. The catcher was expecting a curve and the pitcher threw a fastball, and it splintered the catcher's finger. The other catcher was in the outfield. Cum Posey, the owner of the Grays, saw young Gibson in the stands, so he asked him to stand in as a catcher.

Judy Johnson was on the field that night. "We had to hold the game up until he went into the clubhouse and got a uniform. And that's what started him out with the Homestead Grays." Gibson didn't get a hit that night, but he didn't make an error and that im-

Josh Gibson started playing for the Homestead Grays in 1930.

pressed Cum Posey enough to offer Gibson a permanent spot on the team. Gibson, who stood six feet one and tipped the scales at 214, caught for the Grays for the next two years.

Rarely will anybody argue that Gibson was a strong and polished batter, but many questioned his strength as a catcher. Some say he was "adequate," while others, like Roy Campanella, who was himself an outstanding NNL catcher, said he was "not only the

Roy Campanella crossed over from Negro League team
Baltimore Elite Giants to the Brooklyn Dodgers before he was
tragically paralyzed.

greatest catcher but the greatest ball player I ever saw." Between the two extremes was an assessment made by Jimmie Crutchfield, an outfielder who was Gibson's friend.

"I can remember when he couldn't catch this building if you threw it at him. He was only behind the plate because of his hitting. And I watched him develop into a very good defensive catcher. He was never given enough credit for his ability as a catcher. They couldn't deny that he was a great hitter, but they could deny that he was a great catcher. But I know!"

In 1932, Gibson was lured to the Pittsburgh Crawfords where he teamed up with Satchel Paige. He wore the Craw's uniform for five seasons, then he returned to the Grays in 1936. After returning from the Dominican Republic, Gibson rejoined the Homestead Grays and helped them win the 1937 Negro League championship.

Some say his home run record would have been better if he hadn't played for the Grays. That year the Posey Brothers took on a partner, Rufus "Sonnyman" Jackson, a racketeer from Washington, D.C. See Posey remained the business manager and Cum the road manager. They decided to play the Grays schedule half a year at Forbes Field in Pittsburgh and the other half at Griffith Stadium in Washington.

Forbes was known for being a tough home run field, but Griffith was often called "the hitter's graveyard" because its left-field foul line was 407 feet away. "The coffin corner," which was center field, was 427 feet away with a thirty-foot wall. Babe Ruth only hit 34 of his 714 home runs there.

Baseball writer John B. Holway stated in *Josh and Satch*:

> *"If Babe had played all his home games [at Griffith] instead of in Yankee Stadium, he'd have hit more like 400 homers instead of 714 and would have come nowhere close to 60 homers in one year. Though Josh's new park didn't entirely stop him, it must have hurt him considerably."*

Those who knew Gibson in the 1930s said he was playful and loved to clown around. Garnett Blair of the Homestead Grays told Bruce Chadwick in *When the Game Was Black and White* that he saw Josh Gibson hit a home run into the right-field upper deck at Yankee Stadium with one hand. "He was clowning around," Blair explained, "and the pitcher threw him a change-up that he knew was coming. He just held the bat with one hand, swung hard, and knocked it up there. The crowd gasped. Josh, he just laughed his head off."

Gibson said his favorite park was the old Polo Grounds in New York with a 279-foot run down the left-field line, and 257 feet down the right side. But center field was a walloping 505 feet out! Gibson hit a center-field home run there that went "out of the park"!

"No greater hitter ever held a bat," said Buck Leonard, another player for the Homestead Grays.

If Gibson can be compared to Babe Ruth, then Walter "Buck" Leonard can be compared to the great Lou Gehrig, the New York Yankees' first baseman known for his hitting ability. Leonard posed a threat every time he approached the plate. Leonard, who was a left-handed hitter, stood five feet eleven inches tall and weighed 185 pounds. His power and consistency at the plate earned him an impressive .341 career batting average, just slightly under Gibson's. Most experts agree that Leonard was a very gifted first baseman.

Gibson was the undisputed king of home runs, but he could be struck out. Leonard was sure to get a hit off of the best pitchers in the league, including one of Satchel Paige's fastballs. Leonard could knock balls out of the park, too, but he was better known for base hits and runs batted in (RBI's).

Leonard didn't start playing professional ball until he was almost twenty-five years old. Born in North Carolina, September 8, 1907, Buck quit school at age fourteen and went to work in a stocking factory. He shined shoes and worked in the train yard of the At-

Left-handed hitter Buck Leonard retired with a .341 career batting average.

lantic Coast Line railroad. Then, for the next nine years, he played ball with a variety of semipro teams along the East Coast. They weren't wasted years, because he was mastering his skills as a hitter and first baseman.

His chance at playing professional baseball came while he was playing with the Brooklyn Royal Giants in 1934. Smoky Joe Williams, who was working at a nearby bar, asked Buck if he wanted to play with a good team.

Buck said he answered, "What are you talking about?"

"The Homestead Grays," Williams responded.

Buck didn't think he had a chance to make the team since he was already twenty-five years old.

Williams told him it wouldn't hurt to try. "I'm gonna call Cum Posey, the owner, tonight and see what he says. I've seen you play two or three times and I think you can make the team."

The following day, Williams told Buck he had called Cum. "He's going to send some money for you to come to Wheeling, West Virginia, for spring training. I'm supposed to buy your ticket and give you some spending money."

From the spring of 1934 Buck Leonard wore a Homestead Grays uniform, and for seventeen years never missed a payday. When Josh Gibson came to the Grays in 1937, he and Leonard became the most feared batting combination in black baseball and they made the Grays the most celebrated team in the Negro Leagues, winning nine straight pennants between 1937 and 1945.

In 1939, the Baseball Hall of Fame was opened in Cooperstown, New York, but no black players were inducted.

CHAPTER

8

Foul Ball

DURING Franklin D. Roosevelt's presidency, there was some progress made in civil rights. But most of the thirteen million African Americans in the United States still were denied basic human rights. They were citizens who were expected to pay taxes, obey laws, serve in the military, but in many places they couldn't vote, serve on juries, or use public facilities. In the 1930s, southern blacks lived under a social and economic reign of terror, led by lawless organizations such as the Ku Klux Klan. Fleeing the tyranny of ignorance and poverty, black families sought relief by moving to large urban centers in the North and Northeast. But the system there was no less oppressive. In the South, hotels, restaurants, and public facilities were clearly marked with the humiliating message:

No Coloreds Allowed or For Whites Only. In the North, there were no such signs, but blacks were nevertheless discriminated against on a regular basis, especially in sports.

The African-American runner Jesse Owens had represented the United States at the 1936 Olympics in Berlin, where he put Hitler's "master race" to shame by bagging four gold medals. But back in the United

Jesse Owens won four gold medals for the U.S. Olympic team in 1936 while baseball remained segregated.

States, whites still insisted that blacks weren't capable or disciplined enough to compete in the major leagues.

All kinds of excuses were used for not including blacks in major league sports. For example, a white major league manager said black baseball wasn't organized. To which Buck Leonard responded, "Oh yes, we were organized. We just weren't recognized!" Blacks were fighting for recognition in government, education, and sports. Even before World War II, blacks were beginning to chip away at the barriers that kept them out of major league ball. But progress was slow.

Locked out of mainstream sports, black baseball teams were forced to barnstorm from city to city, playing whoever would play them. While white players traveled by train, black teams traveled in old cars or buses. White players ate in restaurants of their choice and lived in decent hotels. Black players often ate cold sandwiches, lived in third-rate hotels, or slept on the bus. Sometimes they rode all night, slept on a bench in the park, then got up and played, then back on the bus and on to the next city.

Life was hard on the road. The players who lived through it look back at their experiences sometimes with humor, sometimes with anger, but always with pride. "We were good at what we did," said Cool Papa Bell.

The NNL players — now in their seventies, eighties, and nineties — are eager to pass on their stories to a generation who never got to see them play. These stories are as unique as each player and as diverse as their playing styles. This, then, is what some of them remember about barnstorming in the 1930s and 1940s.

Buck Leonard (Homestead Grays):

"Sometimes we'd stay in a hotel that had so many bedbugs you had to put a newspaper down between the mattress and the sheets. Other times we'd rent rooms in a YMCA, or we'd go to a hotel and rent three rooms. All the ball players would change clothes in those three rooms, go to the ballpark and play a doubleheader — nine innings the first game, seven innings the second game.

"The second game would be over about 6:15. We'd come back to the hotel and take a bath, then go down the street and eat and get back in the bus and go to Pittsburgh . . . get there about 7:30 in the morning, go to bed, get up around three o'clock, go up the river somewhere about twenty-five or thirty miles, play a night game, come back. Next evening, the same thing. We logged thirty thousand miles one summer."

Josh Johnson (Cincinnati Tigers):

"In 1935, we rode to games in cars, but in '36

Discrimination made traveling extremely difficult for players, who frequently had to sleep and eat in their buses.

we bought an old Studebaker bus that belonged to the musical group, the McKinney Cotton Pickers. The brakes weren't much. You had to shift down to stop it. I know . . . I drove it.

"A lot of times we couldn't go in restaurants, because of our color. So we'd make poor boys. We'd stop at a grocery store, get a big chunk of cheese, some lunch meat, some onion, a loaf of rye bread, a couple of cans of sardines — all the guys had pen knives — and pass it around."

Ted Page (Crawfords and Homestead Grays):

"I recall playing baseball in Zanesville, Ohio,

the Middle Atlantic League team. . . . We played in their (whites) ballpark, and there wasn't a man on their team that could have won a spot on the Pittsburgh Crawfords . . . but we couldn't change clothes or take a shower in their clubhouse. Why? We were black."

Ted "Double-Duty" Radcliffe of the Birmingham Black Barons and the Kansas City Monarchs believed that the three greatest owners-managers in the Negro Leagues were the Posey brothers, J. L. Wilkinson, and Abe Saperstein, who was an officer in the Cleveland Cubs Organization and President of the Negro Midwestern League. Radcliffe knew them well, because he'd swung a bat for all three.

They were the only ones, according to Radcliffe, who had four or five sets of uniforms, where most of the other teams had only two. These owners also paid "riding money," which meant that if the team had to stay up all night on a long bus ride, they got their room rent just the same. None of the other teams did that for their players.

Buck O'Neil of the Monarchs echoed Radcliffe's praise of J. L. Wilkinson. According to O'Neil, very few, if any, Monarchs ever got into street fights, shot craps on the bus, or caused disturbances.

The Poseys were known for sticking by their players, but they didn't allow stealing or cheating. These two offenses meant an automatic cut from the squad.

Sometimes, players were challenged by fans who recognized them in public places. Most of the time these kinds of confrontations turned out to be no more than what the players called "selling wolf tickets," which meant bluffing, "talking tough, but taking no action." But sometimes, players got into scrapes that were deadly.

The tragic story of Porter Moss summarizes the dangers black ball players faced each time they went out on the road. Moss's teammates told what happened to Cincinnati reporter John Erardi.

Porter Moss, a pitcher in the NNL from 1934 to 1944, was a strong right-hander known as Ankle Ball Moss. He was "a college-educated man with a long life ahead of him," according to teammates Verdel Mathis and Martin Carter. Moss was by their accounts a fun-loving, all-around nice person, who lived to play baseball and was a good basketball player, too.

In 1944, Moss was with the Memphis Red Sox when their bus broke down. Verdel Mathis said the bus driver couldn't fix it, and they had a doubleheader coming up. So they made arrangements to complete the trip by train. The whole team crowded on the coach reserved for blacks. As soon as the train pulled out, an intoxicated man began harassing several women travelers. Moss asked him to stop. Angry words were exchanged. When the train stopped, the man hopped off quickly, turned, and shot into the crowd. Moss caught a bullet in his chest.

"We carried him to the baggage department and laid him down," said Mathis. "We were told there was a doctor at the next station. When we got there, he said he wouldn't treat Moss because he was colored. We had to go to the next station in Jackson [Tennessee], where there was an ambulance waiting for us. It was about an hour down the line. By that time, Moss had lost too much blood. The doctors operated, but he died that next day." The man was convicted of murder, but sentenced to only ten years in prison.

Remembering his friend, Mathis said, "Moss was at the center of it all. He was the best of it all. I've never met anybody like him. I don't expect I ever will."

Many of the NNL players had definite opinions about who the "best" players among them were. Hilton Smith, a well-respected Kansas City Monarch pitcher, named this dream team:

"I'd pick Buck Leonard as the best first baseman I ever saw. Martin Dihigo at second. Willie Wells shortstop. At third base I'd pick Kenny Keltner of Cleveland. In the outfield I'd put Sam Chapman, and Charlie Keller of the Yankees. Catcher, of course, is Josh Gibson. Pitching staff? I'd have to go with Lon Warneke of the Cubs. Ooh, that

*boy could pitch! And Bobby Feller, of course,
and Bob Lemon, and Raymond Brown of the
Homestead Grays. And yeah, oh, yeah, I'd put
Satchel in there too."*

It is doubtful that two NNL fans would agree with
Hilton's selections, especially his pitching choices.
There was — and continues to be — a running dispute
among the players about who was the "best" at his
position — especially pitchers.

For example, Crush Holloway of the Baltimore
Black Sox said Satchel Paige "was the toughest pitcher
I ever faced." Most people agree, but not Judy Johnson. "Satchel was fast," he said, "but Rogan was
smart." Monarch pitcher Chet Brewer agreed, but
added, "Smoky Joe Williams was next in my book.
Both were better pitchers than Satchel."

When asked if "Bullet Joe" Rogan might have been
better than him, Satchel answered, "I never did see
him in his prime, if you want me to tell you the
truth. . . . He could throw hard as Smoky Joe Williams — yeah. Oh, yes, he was a number-one pitcher,
wasn't any maybe so."

Buck Leonard, who faced most of them as a batter,
singled out Webster McDonald of the Philadelphia
Stars for his pitching ability. "[McDonald] had good
control. Wherever your weakness was, he'd throw the
ball there."

Then there's Ted "Double-Duty" Radcliffe who

Satchel Paige's showmanship and pitching skill made him one of the most famous Negro League players.

lived up to his nickname and earned the respect of his teammates, white major-leaguers, and fans when he pitched a 3–1 victory with a broken finger! "I could only use three fingers," he said. "So I did what I had to do."

The stories are endless, and so are the discussions.

Even today, the debate goes on. Another topic that can get a good conversation started among Negro Leagues fans and historians is how the game was played.

Although there were only a few qualified black umpires in the Negro Leagues, they knew how to handle most situations that flared up on the field. When black umpires weren't available, whites were used. Sometimes games were held up because they couldn't find an umpire, and when they did they were often high school coaches or college umpires. According to one story, a Negro Southern League game in Texas was umpired by the county sheriff to keep disappointed fans from rioting.

Fights between players and fans weren't tolerated, because managers didn't take too kindly to losing a paying customer. Besides, if a black hit a white in the South — for any reason — it could cost him his life. But enduring the insults and name-calling was too much for a few of the players and they hit back.

Sometimes the game got rough. Tempers flared and fights broke out on the field, especially when a pitcher deliberately hit a batter or a runner spiked a base man.

"We were out there to win," said Buck Leonard. Black players knew all the tricks of the trade and used them. Major league rules forbid pitchers to "alter the ball" by applying grease, spit, or any other substance. In the NNL there was no such restriction. "Everything was legal," said Cool Papa Bell, "which meant we had to play harder and smarter to win. . . . We did what we had to do to win games."

Not all clubs allowed rough play. The Kansas City Monarchs, for example, insisted that the players hold high standards of living on and off the field. Coming to the field intoxicated meant an automatic suspension, and a Monarch was stiffly fined for spiking and fighting. But nobody could control the players' mouths.

"Oh, they talked so bad to you." Bell explained how the NNL catchers had a practice of saying things to the batter to "psych" him out. The pitcher did it, too. One trick was to yell the name of a batter's girl-

The Kansas City Monarchs held their players to a high moral code of conduct.

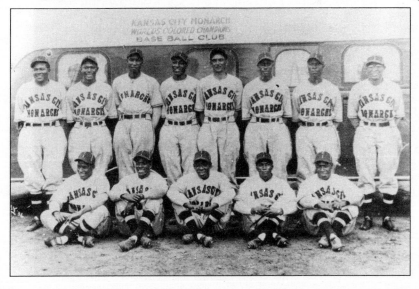

friend just before releasing the pitch to break the batter's concentration. "Now you never called a player's mama's name or his wife. That would get you in serious trouble, but girlfriends — that was fair game," said Bell. "Who said we didn't have rules?"

Pitcher Ted Radcliffe talked with writer John Holway about the sliders.

"The roughest sliders were men like Turkey Stearns and Newt Allen, and I never did get cut by them (with cleats). Now the greatest slider there ever was in baseball was this Crush Holloway. He jumped at me once, and then when I caught him at the bat when I was pitching in Cleveland, I knocked him down twice. He said, 'Are you trying to kill me?' I said, 'I'm trying to make a living out there, but you trying to kill me when you came home.' That night we went out and had some beer. That ended it. He never jumped anymore, I never threw at him anymore."

It was not common for pitchers to deliberately hit a batter to avoid risking a hit or possible home run. "Best to go on and hit him [the batter] on the first pitch," said Paige. "That way you don't have to wear your arm out."

Ted Page, who had a notorious reputation for spiking, admitted that pitchers often threw at him. Page told a story about how Martin Dihigo got his revenge.

"I remember," Page said, "one day when I was with the Brooklyn Royals, Martin Dihigo was playing shortstop. I slid into him, and you know how I slid, I undressed him . . . Next day, Dihigo pitched. He threw at me — I don't mean he threw high, I mean he threw at me . . . When we'd play the Cubans," he added, "they would always throw at me. See that spot on my temple? No hair. The guy hit me there was a Cuban, in Palm Beach."

"You had to be tough," said Willie Wells, who was manager of the Newark Eagles. "You had to have heart, desire. If you were a coward, they'd throw right here at your ear. We were playing in Yankee Stadium one day against Satchel Paige. I came to bat. Satchel walked off the mound and reached in his pocket like he had sandpaper. I said, 'What are you doing that for, you got such a good fastball?' He said, 'I'm gonna stick it right in your hair' . . . That's the way they played. You didn't play easy like these guys now."

CHAPTER

9

Away Games

IN South America, the Caribbean, and Mexico, black players were treated with respect and dignity. For Cool Papa Bell that was reason enough to play south of the border. "Everybody was the same down there," said Bell, who played winter baseball in Cuba in 1928–1930, the Dominican Republic in 1937, and Mexico in 1938–1941. "We could go in any restaurant, stay in hotels, and oh, the fans? They loved us."

Some of the best players were invited to play winter ball in Cuba, Puerto Rico, the Dominican Republic, and Mexico. The only difference was that there was no segregation. Jim Crow didn't fly too well outside the United States. One of the ways blacks got to measure their skills against white players was in Latin America. Except for exhibition games organized by

The Cuban All Stars in 1942.

players like Dizzy Dean and Babe Ruth, blacks never got to prove themselves in actual games.

According to Bell, many of the white players were surprised when they found out that they had to play against blacks. "Some of the white boys didn't want to play against us down there. But the Cubans said, 'We all play together here. It doesn't make any difference.'"

Bell's record was just as impressive in the Latin American leagues as it was in the States. He hit a cumulative .378, stole sixty-nine bases, and racked up twenty-nine home runs. "He was a hero down there," said Buck Leonard. "He did so well, a lot of the boys thought they'd take a look for themselves."

Actually, Bell was following the lead of the Cuban X Giants who were the first all-black team from the United States to play in Cuba during 1900. The X Giants won fifteen games on that tour and lost only three. The X Giants visited Cuba again in 1903 and went 9–2.

Cuba began its first winter league in 1907 with a season running from December or January to early April. It was a chance to earn money during the off-season and a chance to play all year. The Cuban winter league was not disbanded until 1959 by order of Fidel Castro.

Rube Foster's Leland Giants packed off for Cuba in the fall of 1910. Foster was amazed that they "encountered no color barrier, no discrimination, no segregated seating, no Jim Crow." That was also the same year the Havana team embarrassed the American League champions — the Detroit Tigers.

The Tigers came to Cuba with the renowned base stealer Ty Cobb, who hit .385 that year. Havana borrowed the Leland Giants pitcher John Henry "Pop" Lloyd. They knew how good he was, but the Tiger champions were full of themselves.

Cobb, a southerner, was known for being mean-spirited and for spiking players. His dislike for blacks was also well known. Lloyd, on the other hand, was good-natured, a gentleman off the field, but he was not to be taken for granted. He was a fierce competitor on the field.

Cobb arrived in Cuba for the fourth game in the series. The Tigers were up two games to one against Havana. In the fourth inning of the fourth game, Cobb was on first. Lloyd was playing shortstop that day. Cobb was an excellent base-stealer, so Lloyd was prepared.

Ted Page explained, "If you slid in with a hook slide (like Cobb), you'd get your shins torn up, because

Ty Cobb, a major league player, was known for his racist comments about black players.

he'd stick those 'stilts,' as he called them, down between you and the bag, and there was no way to get in there."

The "stilts" that Page talked about were cast-iron shin guards. So, when Cobb tried to steal second with a hook slide, spikes up, Lloyd put a stilt out. Havana went on to beat the Tigers, 3–0.

Havana and Detroit tied the series at six games each. Cobb played five games that November, and he hit a .369, but with no stolen bases. Cobb was so upset he promised never to play against blacks again.

Lloyd, nicknamed *El Cuchara* (the spoon) because he had such big hands, was a Cuban sports hero from that game on, always welcome in Havana. But while the Leland Giants were enjoying fame in a foreign country, race riots broke out in Texas and Oklahoma as a result of Jack Johnson, a black heavyweight, successfully taking the title from Jim Jeffries, the Great White Hope.

Playing ball in Latin America meant more than earning more money, getting a chance to play against white players, or even the respect players were shown. For many players it was a chance to play a regular schedule without having to ride long distances, sleep on benches, and eat cold food. Also, the press recognized their accomplishments and wrote feature stories about them. Although many of the players couldn't read Spanish, it was important to them to be recognized. That never happened in the States, except in

Jack Johnson was heavyweight champion from 1908 to 1915.

black newspapers. For the most part the mainstream press ignored black achievements.

It was no wonder, then, that the 1937 raid on the Negro Leagues by General Rafael Trujillo of the Dominican Republic was so successful. Playing south of the border was part of most Negro Leagues' players off-season schedule.

Bottom of the Ninth

WHEN the United States entered World War II, jobs opened up in munitions plants and factories. Though jobs were plentiful, black unemployment was still at Depression level. While black soldiers were fighting for democracy in Europe and in the Pacific, back home their parents were being discriminated against. Plants put out signs welcoming "ALL WORKERS EXCEPT GERMANS, ITALIANS, AND NEGROES."

In January 1941, before the war began, civil rights leaders had taken action to try to avoid this. A. Philip Randolph, president of the Brotherhood of Sleeping Car Porters, the first black union admitted to the American Federation of Labor (AFL), along with Walter White of the NAACP, and T. Arnold Hill, acting

Black aviators trained for World War II in the face of persistent segregation.

executive director of the Urban League, called for one hundred thousand blacks to march on Washington, D.C., to protest discrimination in government defense programs.

The march wasn't necessary. On June 25, 1941, President Roosevelt signed Executive Order 8802, which stated that racial and religious discrimination in government training programs and defense projects was forbidden.

That opened up government jobs for black Americans who, in turn, put money into small black businesses. It was a very good time for black baseball, so good that the NNL lost only one baseball team between 1942 and 1948. But the Negro Leagues were still not without their problems.

Rationing of food, gas, and other things during the war was a way of life. Americans willingly made sacrifices the government told them were necessary. But, in 1943, the Office of Defense Transportation (ODT), the governmental department that rationed gas, began discussing the possibility of prohibiting bus travel. A ban on bus travel would have inconvenienced the major league teams. To the black league teams, who depended so much upon barnstorming, the ban would have been disastrous. Nobody wanted to look unpatriotic, but both black and white baseball protested the decision. The ODT eventually decided against the order and baseball survived.

Another drain on baseball was the loss of players. So many of the young men volunteered or were drafted for service. So the leagues depended upon the older players — Paige, Leonard, Gibson, and Ray Dandridge, who were too old for the Army — to keep the leagues going.

Owners also had to make some innovative changes. Several teams arranged barnstorming tours near military bases where they played against military squads.

These games provided entertainment for the stateside troops, and also helped to keep the morale high among the soldiers.

Some owners recognized women's teams and barnstormed, playing exhibition games against hometown teams or factory squads before the men's competition. By that time, night games had really caught on, so games were scheduled around the clock to accommodate workers' shifts. And, during the war years, black baseball saw the return of the clown teams.

A lot of black baseball owners resented the performances of the clown teams because, in their opinions, the players only reinforced the age-old stereotypes that Rube Foster had fought so hard to dispel. Many ball players didn't think the acts were demeaning, however. "Black baseball was colorful," said Othello Renfroe, a former Kansas City Monarch.

The Indianapolis Clowns were at least one team that had mastered the combination of showmanship and good baseball. In the 1940s, they had Reece "Goose" Tatum (who later played basketball with the Harlem Globetrotters) and King Tut to do an act before the game or between innings. Renfroe described it:

"[Tatum and Tut] would go through a tooth-pulling act where Goose was a dentist and Tut was a patient. Tut would fill his mouth up with

corn. Goose would try to pull the tooth but without success. Then he'd put a firecracker in Tut's mouth and when it exploded [safely] Tut would spit out the corn like he was spitting out teeth.

"They kept you in stitches."

Oscar Charleston (center with Clowns), King Tut (right), and Connie Morgan "Peanuts" (left).

But the Clowns also won games and attracted first-class players.

"People loved them," said Renfroe. "They paid the salary for the league, because any team able to barnstorm with the Clowns made money. They packed them in — small towns or large towns, they packed them in."

Although they were very popular, most of the NAL and NNL teams maintained the high professional standards set by Rube Foster back in the 1920s.

During the 1930s, Cum Posey's Homestead Grays and Gus Greenlee's Pittsburgh Crawfords fielded some of the best talent available at the time. But by the end of the decade, the teams had made some significant shifts. In 1938, Gus Greenlee decided to disband his team and invest in heavyweight boxing potentials. He sold his stadium, which was torn down in order to build a housing project. The Homestead Grays moved to Washington, D.C., but continued to lead the NNL, and the Kansas City Monarchs had moved over to the Negro American League. In 1940, the NNL teams were:

- Homestead Grays
- Baltimore Elite (pronounced EE-light) Giants
- Newark Eagles
- New York Cubans
- Philadelphia Stars
- New York Black Yankees

The 1940 Negro American League teams were:

- Kansas City Monarchs
- Cleveland Bears
- Memphis Red Sox
- Birmingham Black Barons
- Chicago American Giants
- Indianapolis Crawfords

The two dominant teams during the war years were the NAL Monarchs, managed by the legendary J. L. Wilkinson and the NNL Newark Eagles, owned and managed by Abe and Effa Manley.

One of the most famous teams in the Negro Leagues was the Newark Eagles owned by Abe and Effa Manley. The Eagles was one of the teams in the country to be managed by a woman. Abe Manley, a very wealthy numbers man, organized the team in 1935, and his wife, Effa, managed it. By all accounts she was as tough as nails and just as sharp. As important as Effa was to the team, she always credited her players and her husband with their success. "It was Abe's money that got the team off the ground," she said. "He kept the money coming."

Manley, a very fair-skinned woman whose father was black and mother was Scandinavian, could have passed for white, as some blacks did and still do. Effa

Effa Manley worked diligently to support and develop the Negro Leagues.

Manley, however, chose to be black and took an active role in civil rights causes.

She was aware that blacks had made some advances during the war. But, in May 1943, riots erupted in Mobile, Alabama, because twelve black factory workers were given better positions than whites. The Ku Klux Klan, hooded in white sheets, torched black homes and businesses and brutalized innocent men and women. Before the year was over, there were race riots in Beaumont, Texas; Detroit; and Harlem. "Our boys were fighting for other people's freedom, and they weren't even free themselves," said Effa Manley.

Known for being a woman of action, she held antilynching days at the ballpark and was a member of the National Association for the Advancement of Colored People (NAACP). She was committed to any cause that bettered the condition of African Americans, and she made that same commitment to the ball club.

Eagles infielder Monte Irvin praised Effa Manley. "It's too bad the other owners didn't go along with her on many of her proposals. She thought they had to treat the ball players better — better schedules, better travel, better salaries."

Making good on her word, she bought the team an air-conditioned bus, and the Eagles were paid some of the best salaries in the Negro American League. When players retired, Ms. Manley continued to be concerned about their welfare. According to Eagles outfielder Lenny Pearson, the Manleys helped get him started in a business by financing his first tavern in Newark, New Jersey. Pearson later became a successful businessman.

Effa Manley tried not to let the fact that she was a very beautiful woman get in the way of her job as manager. But sometimes it did in a humorous way.

According to Eagles player Bob Harvey, Manley's bunt signal caused a few problems. "She'd cross her legs," he said. One batter was so busy watching her legs he forgot the ball was coming, and it hit him in the head and knocked him unconscious.

From 1944–1945, the Eagles were a powerhouse with an enviable lineup — Larry Doby, Monte Irvin, Don Newcombe, and superstar Ray Dandridge.

Infielder Dandridge played ball for sixteen years beginning with the Detroit Stars in 1933, then to the Newark Dodgers, and finally the Newark Eagles. Except for a few seasons in Mexico, where he was a tremendous success, he stayed "in the Eagle's nest." Dandridge was a good defensive and offensive player. Cum Posey said of him, "There simply never was a smoother-functioning master at third base than Dandridge, and he can hit that apple, too."

The "Second Dynasty" of the legendary Kansas City Monarchs began in 1942 when J. L. Wilkinson brought back Satchel Paige, who had been barnstorming with any team he could hook up with. Word was out that Paige's arm was pitched-out, but he could still draw a crowd.

The war, of course, took several of Wilkinson's best players; still, he had no trouble getting good athletes. Being a Monarch meant being on a first-class team and the chance to play with one of the best owners in the league.

Ray Dandridge played both in Mexico and the United States.

Ted "Double-Duty" Radcliffe remembers Wilkinson. "I joined the Monarchs as a catcher after Abe Saperstein pulled out of the Black Barons." Radcliffe was almost immediately hurt. He had to catch a plane and come on to Chicago to get an operation. "I hadn't been with Kansas City but two weeks," he said, "but Wilkinson paid the whole hospital bill. So you know what kind of man he was."

To keep attendance up, Wilkinson scheduled games for war workers on swing shifts, distributed free tickets to GI's, sold war bonds at games, and played benefits for the Red Cross. Along with fresh new talent, he brought in the older, more experienced players who had name recognition. Among them was Satchel Paige.

Paige had almost ruined his arm pitching in the Mexican League, and he was still under a lifetime suspension for leaving the Newark Eagles. Most people thought Paige's career was over. But Wilkinson put him in a Monarch uniform and assigned him to the "B" Team, that barnstormed the small towns while the main teams played the cities.

Paige was very grateful to Wilkie. In his autobiography, *Maybe I'll Pitch Forever*, Satchel said, "I'd been dead, now I was alive again. I didn't have my arm, but I had me a piece of work." Then miraculously, Satchel's arm was all right.

Satchel was back!

Wilkinson quickly cashed in on the popularity of the tall lanky pitcher with the acrobatic windup. Word spread quickly.

Satchel is back!

Between 1937 and 1947, the Monarchs won the Negro League pennant seven times! They won the black World Series in 1942, when they stood down the Homestead Grays and held Josh Gibson's series average to a pitiful .125.

Satchel Paige of the Kansas City Monarchs (right) with David Barnhill of the New York Cubans.

When asked what was the secret of his eternal youth, Satchel answered with the homespun wisdom and humor that had endeared him to millions of fans:

"1. Avoid fried meats, which angry up the blood.
2. If your stomach disputes you, lie down and pacify it with cool thoughts.
3. Keep the juices flowing by jangling gently as you move.

4. Go light on the vices, such as carrying on in society — the society ramble ain't restful.
5. Avoid running at all times.
6. And don't look back. Something might be gaining on you."

Kansas City proved to be a good place for Satchel in more ways than one. Under Wilkinson, Satchel was more controlled and he mellowed out. He was still flamboyant and loved fast cars and sporty clothes, but he was different. One teammate summed up the change:

"He always had fast cars, Lincoln Continentals, tailor-made suits, and plenty of women. But he married this girl [Lahoma] in Kansas City and started raising a family, and he settled down."

Then, in the winter of 1945, Wilkinson got a tip from pitcher Hilton Smith about an Army lieutenant just out of the service. Wilkinson decided to look the young man over. His name was Jackie Robinson.

CHAPTER

11

A Winning Season

BY 1945, the war had ended. Black soldiers, who had risked their lives defending democracy, were no longer content to be second-class citizens. Black workers weren't willing to give their jobs to returning white soldiers. Tensions mounted, but this time many whites were agreeing that segregation should end, and besides, it was becoming an embarrassment to the U.S. Government. The winds of change were shifting in a new direction.

Since the mid-1930s, there had been talk about integrating American sports. The U.S. Olympic teams had been integrated since the 1920s with great success. And college teams were integrated. If it worked there why couldn't it work in major league sports?

A few bold sports writers like Heywood Broun and Jimmy Powers targeted baseball and challenged the unwritten "tradition" of keeping black players out of the majors. "Only one thing is keeping them out of the big leagues," wrote Shirley Povich of *The Washington Post,* "and that is the pigmentation of their skin. They happen to be colored."

Clark Griffith, owner of the Washington Senators, the first one to speak out against the "gentleman's agreement" that had banned blacks from the sport since the National League was founded, made this famous prediction:

> *"A lone Negro in the game will face caustic comments. He will be made the target of cruel, filthy epithets. Of course, I know the time will come when the ice will have to be broken. Both by the organized game and by the colored player who is willing to volunteer and thus become a sort of martyr to the cause."*

Gabby Hartnett, manager of the Chicago Cubs, added this: "If managers were given permission, there'd be a mad rush to sign up Negroes."

Although the critics of segregation were growing in number, there weren't enough of them to overcome the strong opposition that wanted to maintain the status quo. They used these arguments to keep the color line clearly drawn:

1. A large number of major league players were southerners, and they wouldn't play with or against black players.
2. Fans might riot if there was a dispute between a white and black player.
3. The clubs trained in the South. Black players couldn't stay in hotels, and they were forbidden by law to participate in sports with whites.
4. Black players just weren't good enough.

Everybody knew these were hollow excuses, but nobody was willing to rock the boat.

Black players had heard it all before. "We didn't think anything was going to happen," said Buck Leonard. "We thought that they were just going to keep talking about it, that's all. They'd talked about it all those years and there'd been nothing done. We just didn't pay it any attention. We'd say, well, if it comes, we hope to have a chance to play, but we just didn't pay it any mind."

Effa Manley and several other owners hoped that one or more of their teams might be admitted to the white minor leagues. Then managers could move black players into the majors gradually. But Branch Rickey, president of the Brooklyn Dodgers, shocked everybody when he announced at a news conference that he was going to start a new black baseball league to be named the United States League. Manley was suspicious of his motives.

Baseball commissioner Happy Chandler at Briggs Stadium in Detroit in 1915.

"I asked him if he was so interested in Negro baseball," Effa Manley said angrily, "why hadn't he contacted the two Negro Leagues that had operated so long?"

It is not clear whether Manley got an immediate answer or one later, but Rickey was quoted as saying the Negro leagues were run by "rackets" men and "were not recognized organizations." Rickey never followed through on his plans to start a new Negro League. He had other plans. But the battle lines between Effa Manley and Branch Rickey were drawn.

By then, baseball had a new commissioner, A. B. "Happy" Hap Chandler, the former governor of Kentucky. He seemed an unlikely champion of integration, but Chandler told a reporter that "if a black boy could make it on Okinawa and Guadalcanal . . . he could make it in baseball." Chandler wouldn't retract his comment and the press printed it.

Immediately, he was blasted by white owners. A *Sporting News* editorial stated, "Negroes were better off in their own leagues." The paper blamed "agitators who have sought to force Negro players on the big leagues, not because it would help the game but because it gives them a chance to thrust themselves into the limelight as great crusaders in the guise of democracy."

But Chandler's position gave Rickey the green light he needed. On October 23, 1945, Rickey made history by signing a contract with Jackie Robinson to play with the Brooklyn Dodgers. For years people had wondered who the black player would be who would wipe out the color line. Some thought it would be Satchel Paige, others pulled for Josh Gibson or Buck Leonard. Jackie Robinson was a surprise to many.

Why Jackie Robinson?

Ted "Double-Duty" Radcliffe summarized why Jackie was chosen:

"I roomed with Jackie Robinson the two months before he was called up to Montreal to be the first black. I don't think I've met a guy with more class in my life. He was deferential to older players, respectful to all women, kind to kids, went

out of his way to help old people. When he went up I knew he'd go through hell, but I also knew he had it inside and that he'd make it."

Jackie Robinson had all the qualities needed to be the first black man to cross the color line and play major league ball. He had the strength to stand by his convictions and the courage to remain calm under pressure. On and off the field he was an honorable man, kind and honest. It was no accident that he was chosen for the job.

Robinson was born in 1919 in Cairo, Georgia, and moved to Pasadena, California, as a small child. His

Jackie Robinson with Branch Rickey, signing a contract with the Dodgers.

Robinson ran track when he was at UCLA.

family was very poor, but they were never poor in spirit. The family encouraged their sons to play sports. Jackie's brother was on the 1936 Olympic track team with Jesse Owens. All through high school and college,

Robinson was a scholar-athlete. The All-American football star made a reputation for himself at UCLA, in track, basketball, and baseball.

During World War II, Robinson served in the Army in an all-black unit, and was promoted to lieutenant, one of the first black officers in his unit. One day, Jackie refused to ride in the back of a bus. He was arrested and put on trial. Although he was found not guilty by a military court, the stigma of the trial stayed on his record. Wilkinson is credited with being the person who "gave Satchel his second chance — and Jackie Robinson his first."

After the war, Robinson joined the Kansas City Monarchs. Wilkinson's instincts told him he had potential, and during his first year he played well, but not spectacularly. But his intelligence and past accomplishments impressed Branch Rickey.

Rickey invited Robinson to New York. Their conversation was cordial at first, then Rickey began calling Jackie names, vicious names that hurt. Robinson was surprised and shocked at first, but he stayed calm. He said nothing. For several hours Rickey did everything he could to make Robinson angry enough to hit him, but the young black player remained composed. It had all been a test, staged to see how Jackie Robinson could handle himself under pressure.

Rickey told Robinson that if he was going to be the first black to play in the majors, he'd hear all those words, he'd be called all those names. "You're going to need the courage not to fight back," he said. "That's just what they want you to do."

A week after the signing, *The Sporting News* gave this view:

> *"The war is over. Hundreds of fine players are rushing out of the service and back into the roster of organized baseball. Robinson conceivably will discover that as a twenty-six-year-old shortstop just off the sandlots, the waters of competition will flow far over his head."*

Robinson had only played one year with the Monarchs. He needed more experience, so Rickey started him out with the Montreal Royals, a farm team for the Brooklyn Dodgers. It was also a good testing ground for public acceptance of a black player. The 1946 season began on April 18, and Robinson hit a home run during the first game. It was a good start for the Montreal Royals, but of course, every eye was on Robinson. Every time he hit the ball, ran a base, or made an error it was national news. Never before had a farm team gotten so much attention.

The black players and the NNL and NAL owners watched with interest, too. They were all pulling for him, and he knew it. The pressure on Jackie Robinson was tremendous. When he was on the field, he was not just playing for himself, he held the hopes and dreams of every African-American ball player in his hands.

Years later, Robinson said, "Knowing that I had their [the Negro League players] support meant a lot to me."

If Robinson did well, maybe the door that had squeaked open to let him through would swing open for others.

At first, the hate mail was delivered in big bags to the Dodgers' office, sometimes addressed "to the nigger." Letters were sent to Rickey, too, accusing him of being a traitor to white people. But people sent encouraging and supportive letters, too. Robinson got heartwarming notes from schoolchildren, housewives, construction workers, doctors, and baseball fans from all over the world. Each in their own way sent their congratulations and best wishes.

As the first game of the 1947 season approached, Dodger players wrote a letter to protest Jackie Robinson. Rickey wasted no time. He called all the players together and told them that Robinson was going to play for the Dodgers, and whoever wanted to leave could go. They grumbled and mumbled but no more letters were sent.

The Philadelphia Phillies and the St. Louis Cardinals threatened to strike if the Brooklyn Dodgers started Robinson. But once again, Commissioner Chandler stepped in and promised to put them out of the league. That ended the strike.

A few weeks later, the Phillies arrived at Ebbets Field. On April 15, 1947, Jackie Robinson put on a Dodger uniform and ran out onto the field. The crowd was divided — some cheered, others booed. Rich, poor, young, and old, people from everywhere had come to see Robinson play.

Clark Griffith's prediction was on target. As soon as Robinson stepped out on the field, the Phillies started calling him every bad name they could think of, and his Dodger teammates didn't seem to care. They offered him no support either. Robinson made it through the day, but it was going to be a very long season.

Game after game, Robinson was subjected to cruel and hateful racial slurs. Fans spat at him, cursed him, and players tried to spike him. The humiliation and abuse that was heaped on him was more than any one person should have had to endure just to play a game. Yet he took it all with a dignity that demanded respect. Soon the jeers began turning into cheers.

Rickey knew that Robinson was under a lot of pressure and so did his teammates. Jackie Robinson proved that he could take the heat and stay focused. He was a hard hitter, a fantastic runner, and good shortstop, and in spite of it all, he was helping the Dodgers win games. This earned him the admiration of his fellow players.

Jackie Robinson was a superhero, but he was a human being, too. The constant badgering and insults had taken their toll on his spirit. He'd given it his best, but it didn't seem to be enough. One day it seemed as though he might give up. A Dodger teammate, Pee

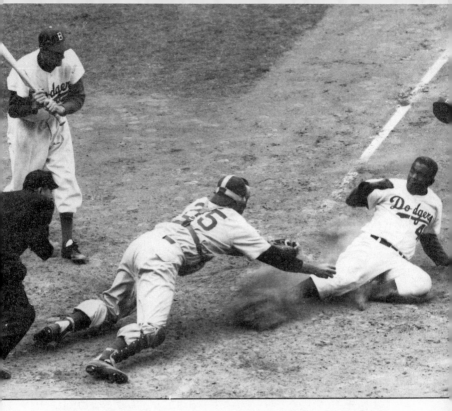

With the bases loaded, Robinson steals home for the Dodgers.

Wee Reese, who was also a southerner, saw Robinson about to crack under the stress. He walked over to him and put his arm around his shoulder and talked to him calmly. A hush fell over the crowd.

This gesture of friendship and sportsmanlike behavior on the part of a southerner sent a strong signal to the rest of the Dodgers, the fans, and the country.

After that day, the Dodgers became a team in the real spirit of the word. Jackie Robinson had accomplished the impossible. The rest is history.

CHAPTER

12

The Close of the Negro Leagues

BLACK baseball had survived the lack of money, the death of Rube Foster, a very rich and well-armed Caribbean dictator, two World Wars, a gasoline crunch, player wars, and racism. But it couldn't survive the major league raids that followed Robinson's success. White teams stripped the black teams of their best players and didn't pay the NAL and NNL owners a dime.

In 1946, the Newark Eagles won the black World Series, but the following year their attendance had dropped drastically because three of their top players had been snatched by the majors. "Without Don Newcombe, Larry Doby, and Monte Irvin, the Negro Leagues had no crowd appeal," said Effa Manley.

She challenged Rickey when he tried to sign one of

Negro National League of Professional Baseball Clubs

Uniform Player's Contract

Parties	The **Newark Eagles Baseball Club** ....
	herein called the Club, and ..**Monty Irvin**..
	of ..**12 Carlton St. E. Orange N.J.**.............., herein called the Player.
Recital	The Club is a member of the Negro National League of Professional Baseball Clubs. As such, and jointly with the other members of the League, it is a party to the Negro National League Constitution and to agreements and rules with the Negro American League of Professional Baseball Clubs and its constituent clubs. The purpose of these agreements and rules is to insure to the public wholesome and high-class professional baseball by defining the relations between Club and Player, between club and club, and between league and league.
Agreement	In view of the facts above recited the parties agree as follows:
Employment	1. The Club hereby employs the Player to render skilled service as a baseball player in connection with all games of the Club during the year ....**1946**... including the Club's training season, the Club's exhibition games, the Club's playing season, any all-star games and the Negro World Series, (or any other official series in which the Club may participate and in any receipts of which the player may be entitled to share); and the Player covenants that he will perform with diligence and fidelity and service stated and such duties as may be required of him in such employment.
Salary	2. For the service aforesaid the Club will pay the Player a salary of $. **700.00**............ per month from ..**May 1st**..... to ..**Sept. 30th**.., as follows:
	In semi-monthly installments after the commencement of the playing season on the .... and .... day of each month covered by this contract, unless the Player is "abroad" with the Club for the purpose of playing games, in which event the amount then due shall be paid on the first week-day after the return "home" of the Club, the terms "home" and "abroad" meaning respectively at and away from the city in which the Club has its baseball field.
	If the player is in the service of the Club for part of the month only, he shall receive such proportion of the salary above mentioned, as the number of days of his actual employment bears to the number of days in said month.
Loyalty	3. The Player will faithfully serve the Club or any other Club to which, in conformity with the agreements above recited, this contract may be assigned, and pledges himself to the American public to conform to high standards of personal conduct, of fair play and good sportsmanship.
Service	4. (a) The player agrees that, while under contract or reservation, he will not play baseball (except post-season games as hereinafter stated) otherwise than for the Club or a Club assignee hereof; that he will not engage in professional boxing or wrestling; and that, except with the written consent of the Club or its assignee, he will not engage in any game or exhibition of football, basketball, hockey or other athletic sport.
Post-season Games	(b) The Player agrees that, while under contract or reservation, he will not play in any post-season baseball games except in conformity with the Negro Major League Rules, or with or against an ineligible player or team.
Assignment	5. (a) In case of assignment of this contract to another Club, the Player shall promptly report to the assignee club; accrued salary shall be payable when he so reports; and each successive assignee shall become liable to the Player for his salary during his term of service with such assignee, and the Club shall not be liable therefor. If the player fails to report as above specified, he shall not be entitled to salary after the date he receives notice of assignment.
Termination	(b) This contract may be terminated at any time by the Club or by any assignee upon five days' written notice to the Player.
Regulations	6. The Player accepts as part of this contract the Regulations printed on the third page hereof, and also such reasonable modifications of them and such other reasonable regulations as the Club may announce from time to time.

Monty Irvin's contract with the Newark Eagles in 1946.

her Newark Eagles. "He had taken Newcombe without saying one word to me," she said. "Now he was coming back for more. I just wouldn't take it. I decided to fight back."

Rickey refused to negotiate with Manley, insisting that the Negro Leagues were not legitimate. When Effa threatened to sue, Rickey dropped the player and leaked the story to the press. Effa Manley was vilified and accused of "standing in the way of her players' progress." Effa wouldn't back down. "I think I sent a message that we weren't going to be robbed of our players without some compensation."

Bill Veeck of the Cleveland Indians bargained with Manley and bought Larry Doby's contract for fifteen thousand dollars. "It would have been one hundred thousand dollars, if we'd been a white team," she said. As hard as she tried, Effa couldn't compete with the money and power of the major league clubs.

In 1947, the Dodgers showed the world that integrated baseball was not only morally right, it was also profitable. The integrated Dodgers and Indians reached the World Series and set all-time attendance records. The Rickey-Robinson "experiment" had worked, so more and more clubs were willing to invest in black players.

In 1948, the Manleys lost Ray Dandridge to the American Association. Although considered among the best infielders to ever play third base, age was against him. Dandridge was in his late thirties when he got his chance, so he never made it out of the minors. But he did make the Hall of Fame for his performance in the Negro Leagues.

The Newark Eagles weren't the only team that lost players, however. The Birmingham Black Barons and the Baltimore Elite Giants also did. The Kansas City Monarchs were the hardest hit, because they had some of the best players. After losing Robinson, they also lost Satchel Paige to the Cleveland Indians.

Cool Papa Bell and Buck Leonard missed the majors because of their age, but the baseball world was saddened by the death of Josh Gibson. When Robinson was chosen over him to play in the majors, Gibson seemed to give up on life. A few say his decline into alcohol and drugs had already started before Robinson broke into the majors, brought on by too many years of trying without recognition.

Gibson started missing games and his personality turned sour. "The happy-go-lucky guy we all loved was already dead before he died," said Leonard. Then one cold January day in 1947, the big guy's heart just stopped beating. The actual cause of his death didn't seem to matter, because those who knew him said he died of a broken heart. However, Satchel Paige finally got his chance to hurl for a major league team.

Paige, like Dandridge, was way past his prime, but Bill Veeck, a longtime admirer, brought Satchel to Cleveland more as a gesture of goodwill, although others called it a publicity stunt. Veeck knew he wasn't

Josh Gibson died in 1947 without ever playing in the major leagues.

getting a fresh, young talent, but he was getting a legend. Even though Paige was the oldest "rookie" to play the game, he was still a joy to watch. It thrilled the fans to see a man his age — well over forty — retiring hitters one after the other.

After Satchel's first season with the Indians, American League president Will Harridge banned Satchel's famous hesitation pitch. "He said I was tricking the batters and umpires," said Paige, "having the batter swinging at balls when all the time I had the ball in my hand, having the umpires calling strikes when the catcher thumped his glove, making them lie."

Paige moved to the St. Louis Browns, a minor league team, in 1950. Three years later he was back on the barnstorming circuit. Paige kicked around baseball until 1968 when at last he "officially" retired and wrote his autobiography, *Maybe I'll Pitch Forever*. Satchel Paige died in 1982 in Kansas City, Missouri.

Although his major league record doesn't show it — twenty-eight victories and thirty-one defeats and an earned run average of 3.29 — Paige made the Hall of Fame for his Negro League accomplishments. He is still considered one of the best to play the game.

The Eagles hung on for a while, but the Manleys finally sold them to a group out of Texas. "Abe never felt he had been robbed of anything," Effa said. "He felt that by letting the boys go for such a small amount he was helping the boys, and that was enough for him. Abe died feeling he had made a great contribution to major league baseball — and he was more interested in that than anything else."

A lot of the older players were passed over, but there didn't seem to be any bitterness among them. Ted Page said:

"I'll say this: I'm not bitter. I think I'm very lucky to be able to say that I played with all the great ball players, with and against . . . Gibson, Satchel, Charleston, Bell . . . by golly, I've got to be lucky to be on a team with men like that."

By 1948, the once magnificent Kansas City Monarchs were almost depleted. "Dad never got paid for Jackie," Richard Wilkinson said. "Rickey never paid anybody for anything. Nothing could be done about it in those days. If you'd raised a voice about money, they'd have said, 'Oh, you're trying to hold a man back.' " Unlike Effa who had written contracts, the Monarchs only had a verbal agreement with Robinson. Actually Wilkinson had no legal grounds to stand on.

But the Monarchs co-owner (and Wilkinson's brother-in-law), Tom Baird, wanted to lodge a complaint with Hap Chandler, the baseball commissioner, but Wilkie talked him out of it. So, while the fans were cheering for the black players who had made it to the majors, they completely forgot to acknowledge Wilkie for his long years of service to the game. Wilkinson, who was seventy-four years old at the time, retired to a nursing home, where he lived until 1964.

At his funeral, former Monarch Hilton Smith said, "It was pretty bad how they treated him. They just took Jackie, made all that money off him, and Wilk-

The Homestead Grays played their last season in 1950.

inson was the man that was responsible for him playing and he didn't get a dime out of it. It was kind of shady, I thought."

The Monarchs lasted until 1955, then the legendary ball club went unceremoniously off the scene.

Cum Posey died in March 1947. The Grays suffered another major loss when Rufus "Sonnyman" Jackson, their financial backer, died. See Posey kept the Grays active, but the team folded after the 1950 season. "The last time I talked to [See] Posey," said reporter Rick Roberts, "he was in his office, almost in tears. On his way to the hospital. He gave me hell: 'How can you write about my ball players being snatched up by a pirate, didn't need a gun, hiding behind freedom for blacks?' He said it was like coming into a man's store and taking the commodities right off the shelf without paying a dime. 'You don't know how much it cost me to build a team . . . I guess I won't live to fight anymore.' " And he didn't.

The last black World Series in the Negro Leagues was between the Homestead Grays and the Birmingham Black Barons in 1949. It seems fitting that the Grays won, because the following year See Posey had died, and the Grays went bankrupt and disbanded.

By 1949, the Negro American League (NAL) was the only organized league for black baseball teams. Attendance was dismal throughout the year, but the Indianapolis Clowns won the Eastern Division while the Kansas City Monarchs won the Western Division.

Although the heyday of the Negro Leagues was over, a few major league superstars got their start playing for the last of the NAL teams. Ernie Banks honed his skills with the Kansas City Monarchs before going to the Chicago Cubs. The New York Giants paid fifteen thousand dollars to the Birmingham Black Barons for a powerful slugger named Willie Mays. And, the record-breaking home-run hitter, Hank Aaron, played for the Indianapolis Clowns before he put on a Boston Braves uniform.

The Clowns were the most innovative club in black baseball during its decline. In 1953, they made history by signing Toni Stone, a woman player. She played four to six innings a game and hit a respectable .243 in a scaled-down NAL.

The NAL disbanded in 1960, but the Clowns, the

Henry Louis "Hank" Aaron signed with the Braves in 1951.

lone survivers of the Negro Leagues, continued to barnstorm as an exhibition team, much like today's Harlem Globetrotters, a basketball show team.

Meanwhile Jackie Robinson played second base for the Brooklyn Dodgers throughout the 1950s. He

Lyle "Toni" Stone played in the last days of the Negro Leagues. Women are still prohibited in the major leagues.

played in six World Series and was voted the Most Valuable Player in 1949. His lifetime batting average was .311, and, in 1962, he added another "first" to his long and successful career, by being elected to the Baseball Hall of Fame.

No Negro League players were in the Hall of Fame, but in the late 1960s the rules were changed so that superstars of the Negro Leagues could get the honor they deserved. Satchel Paige was first, elected in 1971. Josh Gibson and Buck Leonard were inducted in 1972. Cool Papa Bell, Ray Dandridge, Oscar Charleston, Martin Dihigo, Monte Irvin, Pop Lloyd, Judy Johnson, and of course, Rube Foster were added later. At last a few of the players were recognized and included, but there were so many more good players who have not been honored. Until they are, the season will not be over.

Jimmie Crutchfield of the Pittsburgh Crawfords summarizes the pride that was theirs when the diamond was black and they were masters of the ball and bat:

"I have no ill feeling about never having had the opportunity to play in the big leagues . . . There's no use in me having bitterness in my heart this late in life about what's gone by. That's just the way I feel about it . . . I can say I contributed something."

The great Willie Mays.

PLAYER PROFILES

♦

The following player profiles is not a complete listing of all the Negro Leagues players, but rather a sampling of some of the better-known teams and players.

Henry Lewis "Hank" Aaron began his baseball career at age seventeen, playing infield with the Indianapolis Clowns. The powerful hitter was signed by the Boston Braves in 1951 for ten thousand dollars. Aaron broke Babe Ruth's home run record, hitting over 714 home runs during his long career.

Newt Allen, a Kansas City Monarch second baseman, joined the team in 1922. Allen was a favorite with the fans, and four times he was voted one of the best second basemen in the East-West game — 1933, 1934, 1936, and 1941. He was not a strong hitter, but he was a good team player.

Tom Baird was J. L. Wilkinson's brother-in-law and co-owner of the Kansas City Monarchs. He was a booking agent for league exhibition games, too.

Dan and Fred Bankhead were two of five brothers who played in the Negro Leagues in the 1930s and 1940s. Between 1940 and 1947, Dan pitched for the Chicago American Giants, the Birmingham Black Barons, and the Memphis Red Sox. Fred was an infielder for the same three teams between 1936 and 1948.

Dave Barnhill was a pitcher for the Newark Eagles during the 1940s.

John Beckwith was an infielder and manager for numerous teams, from 1917 to 1938, including the Chicago Giants, Chicago American Giants, Baltimore Black Sox, and others.

James Thomas "Cool Papa" Bell was considered the fastest runner in black baseball. He was so fast, Olympic gold-medalist Jesse Owens refused to race him. Bell played until he was forty-three years old and retired in 1946 with a batting average of .429. He was elected to the Hall of Fame in 1974.

Charlie Biot was an outfielder for the Newark Eagles, the Baltimore Elite Giants, the New York Black Yankees, and others during the 1930s and 1940s.

Garnett Blair pitched for the Homestead Grays during the 1945–1946 seasons.

Dave Brown was a left-handed pitcher who played for Rube Foster's American Giants in the 1920s.

Larry Brown of the Memphis Red Sox was highly regarded as one of the best catchers in the 1930s.

Walter Brown organized the League of Colored Baseball Clubs in 1887, but the league folded after only a few months.

Thomas "Pee-Wee" Butts began his career in 1938 with the Atlanta Crackers. Later, he wore a Kansas City Monarch uniform and became one of the most respected shortstops in the Negro American League (NAL).

Roy Campanella was considered one of the best catchers in the business. Before the Hall of Famer went to the Dodgers, he played for the Baltimore Elite Giants, where he already had a reputation for being a power hitter. In fact, in 1944, he was named over Josh Gibson to the All-American Baseball Team, selected by the *Negro Baseball Yearbook*. A tragic accident paralyzed him and brought his career with the Brooklyn Dodgers to an end.

Oscar Charleston had a twenty-seven-year career (including ten years as a player-manager) in the Negro Leagues. It was Charleston who urged Branch Rickey to sign Roy Campanella for the Brooklyn Dodgers after Jackie Robinson was signed. Charleston was elected to the Hall of Fame in 1976.

Francisco "Pancho" Coimbre, a native Puerto Rican, played with the New York Cubans. His skin was considered too "dark" to play in the majors.

Robert A. Cole owned the Chicago American Giants (bought from Rube Foster) between 1932 and 1935. He was also the treasurer of the NNL and the vice president of the Negro Southern League.

Andy "Lefty" Cooper pitched and managed for several teams between 1920 and 1941.

Ray Dandridge played in the Mexican Leagues and the Negro Leagues from 1933 to 1944. His lifetime batting average was .325. Dandridge was elected to the Hall of Fame in 1987.

Martin Dihigo was born in Cuba in 1905. He began his baseball career in 1923, playing in his native country. He also played in the Negro Leagues in the United States. Dihigo, known for his versatility, played almost every position. He was elected to the Hall of Fame in 1977.

Dizzy Dismukes was a pitcher and manager from 1913 all the way through the 1950s. He began as a player for the Philadelphia Giants, then he moved to the Brooklyn Royal Giants and several other teams for the next eighteen years. He was later involved in management.

Lawrence "Larry" Doby played second base for the Newark Eagles until his contract was bought by the American League Cleveland Indians in 1947. He was the first black to play in the AL. He is also a member of the Hall of Fame.

John Donaldson started his career in 1916. Throughout his career he was known for his fluid and accurate pitch. During the 1930s, he hurled for the Kansas City Monarchs and other teams.

Pat Dougherty was a left-hander who pitched before the Negro National League was organized in 1920. His best and last year in pro-baseball was in 1915.

Bill Drake, known as "Plunk," was a Kansas City Monarch pitcher during the 1930s who had a reputation for having a great curveball. He was also known for throwing at hitters.

The **Duncans** — Frank "Pete," Jr., and Frank, Sr. — both played for the Kansas City Monarchs during the 1941 season.

Andrew "Rube" Foster was the owner of the American Giants and founder of the Negro National League in 1920. The Hall of Famer is often called the "Father of Black Baseball."

Willie Foster was a left-handed pitcher who began with the Memphis Red Sox at age eighteen in 1923. He spent most of his career with the Chicago American Giants. He was the brother of Rube Foster.

John "Bud" Fowler, whose real name was John Jackson, was a nineteenth-century versatile player who made it to the minors playing on integrated teams. By 1899, when his career had ended, he was bitter and angry about the exclusion of blacks in the sport.

Josh Gibson was known as the "Home Run King" of black baseball. He hit 972 home runs in his seventeen-year career with the Homestead Grays. He was elected to the Hall of Fame in 1972.

James "Junior" Gilliam played with the Baltimore Elite Giants from 1945 to 1950, when he was signed by the Brooklyn Dodgers as a second baseman.

Charlie "Chief Tokohama" Grant, an early twentieth-century player, tried to break into the majors by "passing" as a Native American.

Frank Grant played second base for the Cuban Giants in the nineteenth century.

"Big" Joe Greene, pitcher for the Homestead Grays, began his career in 1938 with the Atlanta Black Crackers.

William Augustus "Gus" Greenlee was the founder of the second Negro National League and owner of the Pittsburgh Crawfords.

Robert "Bob" Harvey was an outfielder for the Newark Eagles during the 1940s. When the Eagles moved to Texas, he moved with the team and played there until 1950.

Christopher Columbus "Crush" Holloway was an awesome outfielder who played between 1921 and 1939. Known for his powerful bat, his teammates nicknamed him "Crush." A few of the teams he played for were: the Indianapolis ABC's, the Hilldale Club, and the Baltimore Black Sox.

Elston Howard was a St. Louisan who played for the Kansas City Monarchs beginning in 1948. The Yankees signed him in 1951, but he never made it out of the minors. With Kansas City of the American League, Howard maintained a batting average of .331, which included twenty-two home runs and fifteen triples.

Monford "Monte" Irvin began his career as an outfielder with the Newark Eagles between 1937 and 1948. He moved to the Brooklyn Dodgers after Robinson's success in the majors.

George "Chappie" Johnson was a catcher for a number of teams during the 1930s. During the Depression, he formed the "Chappie Johnson All-Stars" and barnstormed throughout Montreal.

Josh Johnson was a catcher and pitcher for the Homestead Grays, the New York Black Yankees, and Cincinnati Tigers between 1934 and 1942.

Mamie "Peanut" Johnson was one of three women who played in the Negro Leagues in the 1950s. (*See* Toni Stone and Connie Morgan.)

William Julius "Judy" Johnson was an outstanding third baseman whose career spanned eighteen years, ending in 1938. He was a player-manager for some of the Negro Leagues' best teams — the Hilldale Club, the Pittsburgh Crawfords, and the Homestead Grays. He was elected to the Hall of Fame in 1975.

Walter "Buck" Leonard spent his seventeen-year career with the Homestead Grays. He rarely batted below .390. He was elected to the Hall of Fame in 1972.

Rufus Lewis pitched for the Pittsburgh Crawfords and the Newark Eagles. He moved with the Eagles to Houston after the team was sold. Later, he played in the Cuban League.

John Henry "Pop" Lloyd compiled a lifetime batting average of .368. Often called "the Black Wagner," Lloyd was elected to the Hall of Fame in 1977.

Richard "Dick" Lundy played shortstop and managed for a variety of teams, during his long career between 1916 and 1948.

James "Jimmie" Lyons was an outfielder for the Chicago American Giants and other Teams between 1910 and 1932.

David "Gentleman Dave" Malarcher was a soft-spoken, scholarly infielder, who was well liked by his teammates on Rube Foster's American Giants. Later he became the Giants' manager. After his retirement he became a poet.

Abe and Effa Manley were the controversial owners of the Newark Eagles (1934–1948).

Verdel "Lefty" Matthis, the southpaw with the Memphis Red Sox, pitched during the 1940s.

Willie Mays, a Hall of Famer, began his career in the Negro Leagues, playing in the outfield of the Birmingham Black Barons. He was signed by the major league New York Giants. He did so well, he was called up from the minors in May 1950, where he started with the New York/San Francisco Giants. Known as the "Say Hey, Kid," he was a popular player as well as an outstanding athlete.

Webster "Mac" McDonald was a hurler for the Hilldale Club, the Pittsburgh Crawfords, and the Homestead Grays in the 1930s and 1940s.

José "Joe" Mendez was a dark-skinned Cuban who was not allowed to play in the majors. He began his career as a pitcher, but changed to shortstop. During the 1920s he was a player-manager for the Kansas City Monarchs. He died in 1926.

Lee Moody was an infielder and outfielder for the Monarchs from the 1920s to the 1950s.

Connie Morgan was a female professional baseball player who got her start with the all-female team, North Philadelphia Honey Drippers. The Indianapolis Clowns signed her, Toni Stone, and Mamie Johnson to play in the 1950s, hoping it would help their slumping attendance. (*See* Toni Stone and Mamie Johnson.)

Porter "Ankle Ball" Moss was a pitcher for the Memphis Red Sox. He was killed by an angry train rider in 1944.

Buck O'Neil began his career in 1937 playing first base with the Kansas City Monarchs. He later became their manager.

Theodore Roosevelt "Ted" Page was a Pittsburgh Crawford with a solid .400 batting average in the 1930s. He also played with a number of other teams, including the Homestead Grays with Josh Gibson and Buck Leonard.

Leroy "Satchel" Paige was probably the best known of all the Negro League players because of his longevity as a player and his uncanny ability to evade questions about his age. His skill as a pitcher along with his showmanship made him one of the most valuable players the Negro Leagues had. He pitched in the majors in the 1950s, far past his prime, but he was still a crowd pleaser.

Leonard "Lennie" Pearson played various positions in the infield with the Newark Eagles and St. Louis Stars between 1937 and 1950.

Bruce Petway was a renowned catcher in the early part of the twentieth century. He began his career in 1906 with the Leland Giants. By 1911, he was catching for the Chicago American Giants. When he retired in 1925, he was a manager-catcher for the Detroit Tigers.

Spotswood "Spots" Poles was an outfielder for the Hilldale Club and other teams in the early 1920s.

Cumberland "Cum" Posey was the owner and road manager of the Homestead Grays.

Seeward "See" Posey, Cum's brother, was co-owner and business manager of the Homestead Grays.

Ted "Double-Duty" Radcliffe was a catcher and pitcher for the Kansas City Monarchs, the Birmingham Black Barons, and other good teams during the 1920s and 1930s.

Richard "Cannonball Dick" Redding was known for his fastball. In 1912, he won forty-three games and lost twelve. After serving in World War I, Redding returned to baseball with the Chicago American Giants. In 1923, he went to the Brooklyn Royals where he pitched and managed until 1938.

Othello "Chico" or "Chappy" Renfroe was born in Newark in 1923, but he played for the Kansas City Monarchs in the 1940s. He was known for being a tough player and a hard hitter.

Jackie Robinson was the first African American in the twentieth century to play in the major leagues with the Brooklyn Dodgers in 1947. He was also the first black to win the Most Valuable Player, the first to play in a major league World Series, and the first black to be inducted into the Hall of Fame.

Neil Robinson was a power hitter with Cincinnati's West End Tigers. In 1931, Robinson was said to have hit a ball so far the city changed the name of the park from West End Park to Neil Robinson Park.

Wilber "Bullet" Rogan was as versatile as the New York Cubans'

Martin Dihigo. He played every position, except catcher, but he is best remembered as a pitcher with a "bullet" fastball. His career (1917–1946) involved coaching and managing. He was even a Negro American League umpire.

Louis "Top" Santop (Loftin) was a catcher, but remembered more for his powerful batting ability. His longest drive was reported to have cleared a fence 485 feet from the plate. Between 1909 and 1926, he played for the Chicago American Giants, Brooklyn Royal Giants, and the Hilldale Club.

Abe Saperstein was the booking agent for several clubs in the 1940s and the president of the Negro Midwestern League.

George "Mule" Suttles broke into professional baseball with the Birmingham Black Barons in 1918. During his long career, which stretched to 1948, he played first base and outfield with the Chicago American Giants, the Newark Eagles, the New York Black Yankees, and the St. Louis Stars, to name a few.

Hilton Smith was part of the famous Kansas City Monarch pitching staff. In 1938, he pitched a no-hitter against the Chicago American Giants. He had a curveball, which was to be feared, and a reputable fastball, too.

Norman "Turkey" Stearns entered professional ball as an outfielder for the Montgomery Grey Sox in 1921. The left-handed power hitter remained a threat on the mound well into the 1940s.

Toni Stone was fifteen when she signed with the Indianapolis Clowns. She was one of several women who played professional ball in the declining days of the Negro Leagues. She also played with the Kansas City Monarchs. (*See* Connie Morgan and Mamie Johnson.)

George Stovey was a nineteenth-century pitcher who played with the Cuban Giants and other all-black teams in the late 1890s.

Nathaniel "Nat" Strong helped start the Eastern League in 1923 to compete with Rube Foster's Negro National League, which had been started in 1920.

Reece "Goose" Tatum was one of the most popular players on the clown teams of the 1940s. He began with the Birmingham Black Barons, then moved to the Indianapolis Clowns. Tatum later became a star with the Harlem Globetrotters, a basketball show team.

Benjamin "Ben" Taylor started as a first baseman in 1910. Throughout his career he played various other infield positions with the Hilldale Club and the Chicago American Giants.

Charles Ishum "C. I." Taylor was the manager and owner of the Indianapolis ABC's in the 1920s. They were called the ABC's because the team was backed by the American Brewing Company.

Arthur Thomas was a catcher for the Cuban Giants in the nineteenth century.

Frank Thompson was a waiter who organized his fellow workers into a team known as the Babylon Athletics, at a Long Island, New York, summer resort, in the late 1880s. The Babylon Athletics soon became known as the Cuban Giants.

Hank Thompson, a Kansas City Monarch, saw action in the famous World War II Battle of the Bulge. When he came home from the war, he was drafted again, but this time to play for Jersey City. Thompson hit a respectable .303 in fifty-five games.

Christobel Torrienti was a Cuban-born outfielder who was one of the power-hitters who helped make Foster's Chicago American Giants invincible during the 1920s.

Quincy Trouppe was the 1936 St. Louis Golden Glove heavyweight champion, but he chose to play professional baseball. During the 1940s, he was with the Columbus Buckeyes as a player and manager. He was known for being one of the most versatile players to come out of St. Louis.

Moses Fleetwood "Fleet" Walker was a nineteenth-century catcher who played on integrated teams during the 1880s and 1890s in Ohio.

Weldy Walker, the brother of Fleet Walker, played for Toledo in the American Association in the late 1800s.

Normal "Tweed" Webb was born in 1905 and played in the Tandy League in St. Louis. Webb is a black baseball historian who wants to perpetuate the Negro Leagues legacy.

Willie "the Devil" Wells began his career in 1923–1924 with the St. Louis Stars, and became one of the most revered shortstops and power hitters in black baseball well into the 1940s.

Chaney White played from 1920 to 1936. His fame as a capable outfielder for the Hilldale Club and other teams was widespread.

Sol White was a player from 1887 to 1926. He was an outstanding hitter and fielder, but he is best remembered for his writing. He wrote the first history of nineteenth-century black baseball. He lived to see Jackie Robinson play his first game with the Dodgers.

James Leslie "J. L." Wilkinson was in baseball from 1909 to 1948. His first team was the turn-of-the-century All-Nations Team; later the team became the Kansas City Monarchs. Wilkinson, one of the few whites in the Negro Leagues, served as secretary of the Negro National League, and he was elected treasurer of the Negro American League in 1937, when the Monarchs changed from the NNL to the NAL.

George Williams, an infielder between 1885 and 1902, was known for being a hard hitter for the Cuban Giants.

"Smoky" (Smoking) Joe Williams was a remarkable pitcher in the early 1900s. He was sometimes called "the Cyclone" because his fastballs were so fast. Later in his career he managed the Hilldale Club.

William "Yank" Yancey was a well-known shortstop for several seasons in the 1920s with the Hilldale Club, the Philadelphia Giants, and other teams.

HALL OF FAME

♦

Negro Leagues' players in the Hall of Fame (* indicates person played in both the Negro Leagues and the majors):

James Thomas "Cool Papa" Bell
Oscar Charleston
Ray Dandridge*
Martin Dihigo
Andrew "Rube" Foster
Josh Gibson
Monford "Monte" Irvin*
William Julius "Judy" Johnson
Walter "Buck" Leonard
John Henry "Pop" Lloyd
Leroy "Satchel" Paige*
Henry Lewis "Hank" Aaron*
Ernie Banks*
Roy Campanella*
Willie Mays*

TIME LINE

◆

Circa 1820s
The *Mayflower of Liberia* sailed from New York City with eighty-six African Americans who were returning to Africa as part of a "Back to Africa" movement. Americans are changing "rounders" into "baseball." The major sports, at the time, were footraces, wrestling, boxing, and horse racing.

1845
The New York Knickerbocker Club organized; they set baseball playing rules; free blacks were not excluded from the game. Integrated teams and competition were accepted.

1857
The National Association of Baseball Players organized. Dred Scott Decision by U.S. Supreme Court denied citizenship to African Americans whether free or slave. Moses "Fleetwood" Walker born in Mount Pleasant, Ohio.

1858
Approximately fifteen hundred people pay fifty cents each to see an all-star baseball game in New York. John "Bud" Fowler is born in upstate New York.

1861–1865

Civil War; Lincoln assassinated; Thirteenth Amendment ratified, abolishing slavery in the United States. African-American soldiers from the South learn how to play baseball; military teams are integrated.

1867

The Brooklyn Uniques beat the Philadelphia Excelsiors for the first "Negro Baseball Championship." The score, 37–24.

1868

Fourteenth Amendment becomes part of the U.S. Constitution — it declares all persons born or naturalized in the United States are citizens and entitled to equal protection of the law.

1869

The Philadelphia Pythians are the first all-black squad to compete against an all-white team, the City Items. The Pythians win, 27–17.

1870

Fifteenth Amendment becomes part of the U.S. Constitution, declares that the right to vote cannot be denied because of race or previous condition of servitude. Football becomes an offshoot of soccer.

1871

The National Association of Professional Baseball Players is organized. The Philadelphia Pythians apply for membership, but they are denied.

1875

Civil Rights Bill enacted by Congress, giving blacks the right to equal treatment in public places and transportation.

1876

Alexander Graham Bell patents the telephone. The National League Professional Baseball Clubs is organized. Fleet Walker plays on varsity baseball team at Oberlin College in Ohio.

1877

U.S. Presidential Electoral Commission rules that Rutherford B. Hayes wins the 1876 election. William Hulbert of Chicago White Stockings elected president of the National League.

1878

Thomas Edison invents the incandescent electric lamp. Fleet Walker signs with Toledo of the American Association, a minor league.

1881

President James Garfield is assassinated. First "Jim Crow" law, which segregated railroad coaches, is passed in Tennessee. Tuskegee Institute is founded, headed by Booker T. Washington.

1883

The 1875 Civil Rights Act is declared invalid by U.S. Supreme Court rulings.

1884

France delivers Statue of Liberty to United States. Weldy Walker, Fleet Walker's younger brother, plays six games with Toledo club before leaving. John Henry "Pop" Lloyd, one of the best Negro League pitchers, is born.

1885

Former president and Civil War general Ulysses S. Grant dies. The Babylon Athletics organizes at a Long Island, New York, summer resort by a waiter, Walter Thompson. Team later changes name to Cuban Giants.

1886

American Federation of Labor (AFL) is founded. Bud Fowler leads Western League in triple hits.

1887

Seventy blacks reported lynched. The International League (IL), a minor league, accepts eight black players, but by July, the IL decides to freeze the hiring of black players. Walter Brown organizes the League of Colored Baseball Clubs, but it folds one week later due to financial problems.

1888

Benjamin Harrison is elected president. Only five blacks remain in the International League.

1890

The Cuban Giants play in the Eastern Interstate League and win the league pennant. The Eastern Interstate League bans black players and black teams after the 1890 season.

1891

The Cuban Giants move to the Connecticut State League.

1892

Grover Cleveland elected president. There are 161 reported lynchings.

1895

Frederick Douglass dies at age seventy-eight. Booker T. Washington makes "Atlanta Compromise" speech. Bud Fowler organizes the Page Fence Giants.

1896

William McKinley elected president. "Separate but equal" railroad accommodations is upheld by U.S. Supreme Court in the *Plessy* v. *Ferguson* case. First modern Olympic Games held in Athens, Greece. No women or black athletes represent the United States. Bert Jones is forced out of the Kansas State League; he is believed to be the last black player to play on an integrated team until the 1940s. Future Hall of Famer, Oscar Charleston, is born.

1898

Blacks fight in the Spanish-American War. Literacy tests and poll taxes are upheld by the U.S. Supreme Court, thus many blacks lose the right to vote.

1899
Six people die when white and black workers riot over jobs at Pana, Illinois, mines. Eight-five blacks reported lynched. Bud Fowler organizes All-American Black Tourists, a barnstorming team.

1900
William McKinley reelected president. The Cuban X Giants are first all-black team to play outside the United States.

1901
McKinley is assassinated. Theodore Roosevelt becomes president. Charlie Grant tries to break into the National League by passing as a Native American.

1903
Orville and Wilbur Wright fly the first airplane at Kitty Hawk, North Carolina. Settlement of Alaskan frontier begins. There is a bitter league war between the National League and the American League. Future Hall of Famer Cool Papa Bell is born in Mississippi.

1905
Lynching continues. The *Chicago Defender*, a black newspaper, is published. Future Hall of Famer Martin Dihigo is born in Cuba.

1906
Sol White, former player, writes *The History of Colored Baseball*. Satchel Paige is born in Mobile, Alabama.

1907
First electric washing machine invented in Chicago. Buck Leonard, future Hall of Famer, is born in North Carolina.

1908
William Howard Taft is elected president. First Model T is manufactured by Ford Motor Company. Jack Johnson is first black to win the world heavyweight boxing championship.

1909–1910

The National Association for the Advancement of Colored People (NAACP) is founded. The National Urban League is founded in 1910. Both organizations push for integration of the Olympics.

1912

Woodrow Wilson is elected president. Native American Jim Thorpe wins Olympic gold medals in the decathlon and pentathlon. The International Olympic Committee strips Thorpe of his medals a year later when it is revealed that Thorpe had played one summer of baseball for pay.

1915

Albert Einstein introduces his general theory of relativity. Booker T. Washington dies at Tuskegee, Alabama. Ku Klux Klan receives a charter from Fulton County, Georgia. Klan violence escalates.

1917

United States enters World War I. Ten thousand blacks march down Fifth Avenue in New York in a "silent parade" to protest lynchings and racial indignities.

1919

There are twenty-six riots during the "Red Summer" of 1919. Jackie Robinson born in Pasadena, California.

1920

Warren G. Harding elected president. Marcus Garvey opens the national convention of the Universal Negro Improvement Association in Harlem. There is a major league game-fixing scandal that damages the credibility of baseball. Rube Foster organizes the Negro National League. The Negro Southern League organizes a few days later. Black teams barnstorm against first Japanese pro team, the Nihon Undo Kyokai.

1921

The American Football Association is organized. The 1920s are known as the "Negro Renaissance" with blacks making many outstanding contributions to the arts during this period.

1922

Union of Soviet Socialist Republics (USSR) is formed. Dyer antilynching bill passes in the House of Representatives by a vote of 230 to 119. Bill was killed in the Senate. C. I. Taylor, manager of the ABC's, dies in Indianapolis.

1923

Calvin Coolidge becomes president after the death of Harding. Marcus Garvey sentenced to five years in prison after being convicted of mail fraud. Football halfback Harold "Red" Grange, also known as the "Galloping Ghost," enters professional football at a record one hundred thousand dollars per year with the Chicago Bears. The Negro League average salary is about seventy-five dollars a week. The New York Yankees move to their own stadium in the Bronx. The Mutual Association of Eastern Baseball Clubs is organized.

1924

J. Edgar Hoover becomes head of what will later be known as the FBI. ABC's baseball club folds. First Negro League World Series between the NNL and the Eastern League.

1928

Amelia Earhart is first woman to fly across the Atlantic Ocean. Tyrus Raymond "Ty" Cobb retires from baseball after twenty-five years, leaving a record for stolen bases. José "Joe" Mendez, star pitcher of the American Giants, dies in Havana, Cuba. He never made the majors because he was considered too "dark."

1929

U.S. stock market crashes, causing widespread panic, followed by business closings and record-high unemployment. Oscar DePriest is sworn in as a U.S. Congressman from Illinois. The Kansas City Monarchs finish first in the NNL.

1930

Over thirteen hundred banks close due to stock market crash. Rube Foster dies December 9 in a mental hospital. Hall of Fame catcher Josh Gibson catches in his first Negro League game.

1931
Nine blacks are convicted of rape in the infamous Scottsboro case in Alabama. Black teams barnstorm to stay alive. Willie Mays is born May 6.

1932
Franklin D. Roosevelt wins the presidency. Charlie "Chief Tokohoma" Grant dies. Cum Posey, owner of the Homestead Grays, organizes the East-West League, but the league folds by the end of summer. W. A. "Gus" Greenlee, a Pittsburgh racketeer, organizes the Pittsburgh Crawfords. Greenlee Field opens April 29.

1933
Gus Greenlee organizes the second Negro National League. The first of the East-West Games is played.

1934
Arthur L. Mitchell defeats Oscar DePriest for his House of Representatives seat, representing a district in Chicago. Hall of Fame slugger Buck Leonard joins the Homestead Grays and plays seventeen years.

1935
Germany passes anti-Jewish Nuremburg laws. U.S. Supreme Court reverses conviction of Scottsboro Nine. Boxer Joe Louis defeats Primo Carnera at Yankee Stadium. Satchel Paige banned from NNL for the season. The Newark Eagles are organized by Effa and Abe Manley.

1937
Pullman Train Car Company of Chicago formally recognizes the first black union, the Brotherhood of Sleeping Car Porters, headed by A. Philip Randolph. Twenty-six percent of black males are unemployed. Negro American League (NAL) started by H. G. Hall. Satchel Paige raids NNL and forms team to play in the Dominican Republic. Pittsburgh Crawfords finish next to last in the NNL.

1938

U.S. Supreme Court rules that the University of Missouri Law School has to admit qualified black students. Joe Louis knocks out Max Schmeling to win heavyweight boxing championship. Satchel Paige is banned from NNL for life. The Pittsburgh Crawfords fold at the end of the season. Greenlee Field is torn down to build a housing project.

1939

World War II begins in Europe. Concert performer Marian Anderson gives Easter concert at Lincoln Memorial in Washington, D.C., arranged after the Daughters of the American Revolution barred her from performing at their Constitution Hall. First Lady Eleanor Roosevelt had resigned earlier from the DAR in protest. The Baseball Hall of Fame opens in Cooperstown, New York; no blacks are included.

1940

German troops occupy Paris. Germany bombs London. Roosevelt reelected for third term. Benjamin O. Davis, Sr., is named first black general in the regular Army. The Homestead Grays win the Negro National League pennant and the Kansas City Monarchs win the Negro American League pennant. No Negro League World Series is played.

1941

Japanese bomb Pearl Harbor; United States enters World War II. War Department announces the formation of the first Army Air Corps squadron for black cadets. President Roosevelt signs Executive Order 8802. The Homestead Grays defeat the New York Cubans, three games to one, in a playoff for the NNL pennant.

1942

James Farmer founds the Congress of Racial Equality (CORE). Future boxing heavyweight champion, Muhammed Ali (Cassius Clay) born January 17, in Louisville, Kentucky. J. L. Wilkinson brings back Satchel Paige to the Kansas City Monarchs and they win the Black World Series.

1944

Battle of the Bulge is fought. U.S. Supreme Court rules that blacks have a right to vote in primary elections in the South. War in Europe ends. The New York Black Yankees finish last in the NNL. The Homestead Grays win the Negro World Series, four games to one against the Birmingham Black Barons.

1945

World War II ends. Jackie Robinson signs with the Kansas City Monarchs. Branch Rickey makes history on October 25, when he signs Jackie Robinson to play with the Brooklyn Dodgers. The Cleveland Buckeyes win the Negro League World Series in four straight games against the Homestead Grays.

1946

Jackie Robinson plays first game April 18 with Montreal Royals, a minor league team that trained players for the majors. Bill Veeck of the Cleveland Indians buys Larry Doby's contract from Newark Eagles; Doby becomes first black to play in the American League. The Newark Eagles win Black World Series; over twelve thousand spectators attend.

1947

President Truman recommends a civil rights section in the Department of Justice and a Fair Employment Practices Commission. Basketball superstar Kareem Abdul Jabbar (Lew Alcindor) is born in New York, weighing twelve pounds and measuring twenty-two-and-a-half inches. Josh Gibson dies. Cum Posey dies. Jackie Robinson, the first black major-leaguer in modern baseball, opens with the National League Dodgers on April 25. Larry Doby is first black player in the American League with the Cleveland Indians. Robinson becomes first black to play in major league World Series. Doby and Robinson win "Rookie of the Year" awards.

1948

Truman wins election. The Birmingham Black Barons defeat the Kansas City Monarchs, four games to three, in a playoff for the pennant. No World Series is played in the Negro Leagues.

1949

Korean War begins. Apartheid policy adopted and enforced in South Africa. Gwendolyn Brooks wins Pulitzer Prize for poetry. Last black World Series played between the Homestead Grays and the Birmingham Black Barons. Homestead Grays win. Jackie Robinson named "Most Valuable Player."

1950

The Homestead Grays are bankrupt and fold. The NNL folds. The NAL remains the only organized league. See Posey dies. The Baltimore Elite Giants defeat the Chicago American Giants in four straight games for the NAL league title. Last of the East-West games played.

1951

National Guard is called out to subdue rioters in Cicero, Illinois, over segregated housing. Hank Aaron joins the Indianapolis Clowns at age seventeen.

1952

Dwight D. Eisenhower is elected president. Tuskegee Institute announces that 1952 is first year in the seventy-one years of tabulation that there were no lynchings reported.

1953

Toni Stone is the first black woman to play in the Negro American League, first with the Indianapolis Clowns and later the Kansas City Monarchs.

1954

Brown v. *Board of Education* Supreme Court decision reverses the "separate but equal" doctrine of segregation. Oscar Charleston dies; he is inducted into the Hall of Fame in 1976.

1955–1962

The Kansas City Monarchs disband in 1955. The Negro American League is dissolved. The Indianapolis Clowns continue to barnstorm. Jackie Robinson becomes first black to be inducted into the Baseball Hall of Fame.

BIBLIOGRAPHY

◆

Bruce, Janet. *The Kansas City Monarchs: Champions of Black Baseball.* Lawrence, KS: University Press of Kansas, 1985.

Chadwick, Bruce. *When the Game Was Black and White: The Illustrated History of the Negro Leagues.* New York: Abbeville Press, 1992.

Dixon, Phil, and Patrick J. Hannigan. *The Negro Baseball Leagues: A Photographic History.* Mattiuck, NY: Amereon House, 1992.

Gallen, David. *The Baseball Chronicles.* New York: Carroll & Graf Publishers, 1991.

Holway, John B. *Blackball Stars: Negro League Pioneers.* Westport, CT: Meckler Books, 1988.

Holway, John B. *Josh and Satch: The Life and Times of Josh Gibson and Satchel Paige.* New York: Carroll & Graf Publishers, 1991.

Holway, John B. *Voices from the Great Black Baseball Leagues.* New York: Da Capo Press, 1992.

Paige, Satchel, and David Lipman. *Maybe I'll Pitch Forever.* Garden City, NY: Doubleday, 1962.

Peterson, Robert. *Only the Ball Was White: A History of Legendary Black Players and All-Black Professional Teams.* New York: McGraw-Hill, 1984.

Rogosin, Donn. *Invisible Men: Life in the Negro Baseball Leagues.* New York: Atheneum Publishers, 1983.

Thorn, John, and Pete Palmer. eds. *Total Baseball*, 3rd ed. New York: HarperCollins Publishers, 1993.

Trouppe, Quincy. *Twenty Years Too Soon.* New York: S & S Enterprises, 1977.

FILM

There Was Always Sun Shining Someplace: Life in the Negro Baseball Leagues. A Refocus Films Production, 1984.

INDEX

♦

Italics indicate illustrations. **Boldface** indicates player profile.